GOD AND THE DEVIL AT SEAL COVE

by
Angus Hector MacLean

1SBN-0-919380-21-2

First Edition

Published by

PETHERIC PRESS

Petheric Press
P.O. Box 1102
Halifax, Nova Scotia

Printed by
McCurdy Printing Co. Ltd.

Acknowledgements

Angus would have wanted to express grateful appreciation to Nan Giesey for the final typing of the manuscript and for her unfaltering faith in its worth. He would also have wanted to thank Richard Gaines for his critical reading and for the corrections he so kindly made. Appreciation is due and gladly acknowledged to Dr. Charles A. Howe, and the New York State Convention of Universalists.

Angus often expressed his appreciation of the help given by his brothers and sisters in recalling their childhood together—often in the Gaelic and with much laughter.

BOOKS BY ANGUS HECTOR MacLEAN

The Idea of God in Protestant Religious Education
    Columbia University 1930

The New Era in Religious Education
    Beacon Press 1934

The Wind in Both Ears
    Beacon Press 1965

The Galloping Gospel
    Beacon Press 1966

PREFACE

This is a true story. It is about Angus Hector MacLean's early boyhood in Cape Breton near the turn of the 19th century. He tells the story to show how life there really was. I suppose that one cannot help but wonder what Angus Mac-Lean did with his life. Perhaps I can tell you something about that.

Since the book tells of his boyhood days, I will begin here with his post-high school times. This was an exciting period before World War I when he was chosen to become a lay preacher riding horseback between farming communities in the Canadian West. He told this story in *The Galloping Gospel*.

He became a medical orderly in the Canadian Army during World War I. He served much of that time close to the front lines in France. After he was mustered out of the army in 1919, he picked up his schooling where he had left off at McGill University. We were married in the spring of 1922 while he was still in his final year in Presbyterian College, McGill. In that year he won a substantial scholarship and, encouraged by one of his professors, decided to go to Teachers College, Columbia University for his doctorate in religious education. Never before had any student elected to choose a university other than Oxford. In the fall we moved our few belongings to New York.

Those were difficult years there at Teachers College. It was six years before his class work was done and his thesis finished. During the last few years he had a temporary position as an instructor, but feeling that it led nowhere, he began job hunting. The outlook was very discouraging. He found nothing in Canada or in the United States. Just as we were at the point of giving up, a position opened in a small theological school at St. Lawrence University in northern New York State. After due consideration we decided that he should take the position. We stayed there for over thirty years.

Angus held high scholastic standards for his classes. One year he had an influx of football boys who always looked for what they called a "pipe" course. He made certain that this didn't happen again. Students came for counselling and often brought other students who needed help. I told Angus that he should set up office hours so that he could have some time to himself, but he preferred not to. His door was always open, he said. One night about one thirty our door bell rang loudly. We grabbed our robes and rushed downstairs thinking it might be an emergency. We opened the door and there stood two students hand in hand. They looked at us starry-eyed. "We have decided to get married and we wanted you to be the first to know," they explained.

In the basement of the Theological School Angus started an arts and crafts shop. Since at this time there was no arts and crafts facilities in the University, the enthusiasm he generated there soon spread to many students and others in the community. "Not because they expected to become great artists," Angus said, "but because they gained satisfaction in creative work." He was never happier than when he was bird-watching, following a trail, or fishing. A cookout and an early morning bird hike became a yearly school event.

About 1950 the beloved dean of the Theological School passed away and Angus was appointed to take his place. A few weeks later the School's only building burned to the ground. After the fire some of the students were standing aimlessly around, wondering what the future held for the School. At that moment the new dean walked by, looking shocked and tired. He simply said "We shall rebuild." One of the students later remarked, "Those words affected me more than many a classroom hour." The next day Angus picked up a piece of stained glass from one of the windows. It portrayed a hand holding a large key—the "keys to the Kingdom". "It has been put in my care," he said.

The School was rebuilt. Students, faculty, people in the community, and many others gave as much as they could. Within two years the School had a beautiful new building that rivalled their fondest dreams.

On Angus' retirement from the Theological School several years later, we went to a large church in Cleveland, Ohio, where Angus became Director of Religious Education. It was to be a retirement job, but he was kept very busy. In addition to performing his church duties, he managed to write three books about his life and philosophy. Although this book is the last of the three, it concerns the earliest part of his life in Cape Breton.

Ruth R. MacLean
April, 1976

God and the Devil were at Seal Cove some time before I was, and they were my familiars throughout my childhood. They came with the Scottish Highland people to live in a forested land that, when cleared, proved to be a land not of milk and honey, but one of stones and thistles, which were things the Highlanders were quite used to. But there were also the blessed hills on which to build their homes and the sea lochs seldom found elsewhere in the western world—a suitable place indeed for a Scottish Presbyterian God, and even for the Devil, who played a necessary role in the drama of life and death. I soon learned that I owed my being to this God and that I was herded into the straight and narrow paths by the Devil for the good of my soul and the peace of the community.

Speaking from another context, I owe my life to chance and to the circumstances that brought my father and mother together. If someone hadn't told Black Neil—the Widow's Son, as he was always called—that Peggy MacRae would make a good wife, and if Neil's faint heart hadn't been served by a most fortunate custom which sanctioned his using a friend to plead his cause with Peggy, I just would not have been. All of which suggests that life, no matter how we love it and cling to it, is an extremely chancy thing.

1

I was the eighth and next to the last in the order in which children came to Neil and Peggy. In our present time a woman would likely call off begetting children long before the eighth, and so I owe my life to accidents of time, custom, individual temperament, and circumstances as much as to biological process. I am so glad that, whatever agency threw the dice, I did turn up, and had the chance to know the Cape Breton God and his Devil, and the wonderful, hard-pressed people who gave them credence.

And why should I write of my insignificant childhood? Because it was the context in which I first had my being. I write not of my life, but of life as it came to me. I am not important, but the life to which I was given is.

Black Neil's father whose name was also Neil, left the little island of Coll on the west coast of Scotland at the time when crofters were evicted to make room for sheep. Some of his family went to Australia—at least one brother and a sister who raised wheat and sheep to their hearts' content. One brother remained in Scotland. All that is known of him in my family is a letter received by my grandfather, written in Gaelic, and only partly translated as follows:

"To J. Neil MacLean, Valley Mills, Cape Breton, Canada.
Dated May 1st, 1854.
Beloved Brother,-

"This letter I am sending you is to advise you that myself and wife [are well] also young family, the same.

"I received two letters from Effie in Australia since the beginning of 'Augher' the first with twenty-five pounds to divide between (?'eniger'). Herself and people were in health of soul, and were giving much praise to the large, wide, and prosperous country. She herself has made seven hundred pounds on the sale of wheat, apart from the last crop. It is rented ground she has. She took a seven-year lease lately. Land to rent is easy to get in that country. There are good wages for workmen, as a stone-mason has between twenty and thirty-five shillings

2

a day, and coal miners receive good wages and good accommodations.

"She said she was writing to [?] whether you received the same or not. Her address Towerhill, Belfast, Victoria, New South Wales. She was advising you to move there. There is no doubt but she would help you to move there if you would be willing to reveal your financial condition to her.

"Alexander will not go, because his wife will not go with him. She is stubborn. Neil—(Bhillibhride) . . . [This must be a nickname] has sold his stock already, making ready to go; he will have some resources of his own.

"It is feared that if a new Laird comes to Coll, many more will be soaking their Ghads. There is a good crop of grain in Coll this year, all except potatoes. It is only eight barrels that I have.

"They are well in 'Haorin' and in 'Avaraich' and throughout the whole country.

"We are without minister, without church and Manse. Write as soon as convenient. Give my blessing to your whole family.

Your brother
Alan MacLean"

[Translator's note: There are two or more broken lines which were impossible to decipher.]

This letter, so far as I know, is the only family document to remain from my grandfather's time. My first reaction to it is one of humorous delight. Gaelic was my mother-tongue, although I never learned to read or write it, and so I recognize familiar Gaelic phrasing: "It is rented ground she has" and "It is only eight barrels that I have" are just sentences my brothers and sisters write to me today. My second reaction is one of sad nostalgia. How many relatives may I have in Australia and Scotland and Lord knows where else? Did Effie marry, and what was her new name? Did Alexander prevail upon his stubborn wife to go, after all? What about Alan's "young family?" No continuing tie connected any of them with the following generation.

My ancestral line was often recited like a nursery rhyme by my father, first names being used exclusively. "Aonghas, MacNeil, ich Neil, ich Ian, ich Donal Ban." That is a somewhat phonetic writing of what meant Angus the son of Neil, the son of Neil, the son of Ian, son of Donald Ban. Ban means blond or light-colored. I gave this good start to an ancestry research concern in Edinburgh to get them started on digging up the family tree. They made a registration charge of £1:1:5, expended all of fourteen shillings and fourpence on the search, and got as far as my great grandfather. Beyond him there seemed to be a confusion of two families. There were so many Johns and Alans and Neils, etc. in one family, totaling fourteen or fifteen, that they gave up the job. My father's "pedigree", as he called it, was just as useful and went a mite further. But considering the cost of the search, I still have hopes.

The foregoing is a meagre offering with which to begin a biography, yet my line is long enough to go back to Adam, like anyone else's. There's one wee thing more to which I am looking forward. A man with whom I worked on a farm when I was eleven and twelve years old told me about "Little-headed Hughie." He was a MacLean warrior of great prowess who must have been treacherously outnumbered, for he died in battle after losing half his head. Ever since his demise he has visited every MacLean when at the point of death, or so it is said. Little-headed Hughie must be trying to tell us something—maybe to say that there could be worse in the family than a man who lost half his head. I have known some people who lost their heads entirely.

Father's mother not only married a MacLean, but was born a MacLean. Beyond that fact I know nothing of her. I remember her wrinkled, work-sculptured face as though it were something in a dream—there is no voice, no word, no incident with which I can associate her. How much more was time a robber then than now, when I could have her voice, her laughter, her stories of the great uprooting, and the flavor of her personality. A minister who visited Coll when I was very young said that a brother of hers had settled in Toronto.

The family dispersion landed Black Neil in Port Hawkesbury on the Strait of Canso, Nova Scotia at the age of one year along with one brother, Ian, three years old, and their parents. They were met there by a young man who carried little Neil on his back the thirty or so miles through the wilderness to Valley Mills where the family had decided to settle. There were no trains. The place was full of woods and bears, and the family almost pulled up their stakes again before they were properly driven in. Next to them a family by the name of Blue was settled. They had a grist mill which made them indispensable to people for many miles around, and were to play an important part in Black Neil's early life.

Three more boys and two girls were born to Neil and Mary. Then, while still in his thirties, Neil died from an infected axe wound—penicillin still hid in the shadows of the next century. The widow's struggle for the survival of her brood is unrecorded, but it must have been heroic and severe.

There is still less known on my mother's side, not even a "pedigree". All I have has been woven together from overheard snatches of conversation. Mother was a MacRae, and that would mean something to Highland people. "The wild MacRaes" of Scotland were just as wild in Cape Breton, by which I mean vital, tough, and full of vinegar. I read somewhere that the clan MacRae were the only people ever to successfully pull a mutiny in the British army. My mother's people were like that—independent and unsubdueable. It was rumored that the MacRaes produced some prominent clergy in the old land, but they seemed to me to be delightfully free from holiness.

Duncan MacRae, my maternal grandfather, settled within ten or twelve miles of Valley Mills at a spot on the lake known as Big Harbor Island, which was separated from the mainland by a narrow canal said to have been dug by the Micmac Indians with their canoe paddles. Duncan came from Kintail or Kintyre—there was always a difference of opinion on this point among his children in later years. Duncan married twice and begot a raft of children—ten boys and four

5

girls, or thereabouts. I never knew how many were of the first marriage, but there must have been a few. This grandfather also died of an infected wound. The clearing of the scrub and forests of the wilderness must have been hazardous to men from a virtually treeless land.

The MacRaes were also handsome people. Two thirds of that mob of girls were beautiful blondes and redheads. The youngest of them, whom I well remember, was so beautiful that as a child I was in awe of her. But my best love was the mother—Grandma to me. She was a MacDonald and had a parcel of MacDonald and MacPhail relatives. She lived until after I left home, and it was when I was saying goodbye to her that I realized how I cherished her. She was the only grandparent of whom I could remember more than a name.

So it was that I had my start about two miles from Valley Mills at Seal Cove, facing a beautiful arm of the lake at the mouth of a stream. Father's brothers, Hector and Dan, settled next to him, one on each side. Hector had married Jessie, who spoke with a strong Lewis accent, and Dan married Mary, my mother's sister, and so his children were my double first cousins. All about them at Seal Cove were other Mac-Leans, most of them distantly related, whose fathers had come from the Island of Mull, the ancestral home of both branches of the MacLean family—the clan Duart and the clan Lochbuie.

We kids had a strong clan consciousness as we grew up; we even fought over the islands our people had come from. Some kids called us Collites and we fought them and called them Mullites. I have a recollection that my father told me that his father was of the Lochbuie people, and his mother of the Duarts, but the mention of this recently brought strong protest from others of my family. We were all Duarts, they thought. I remember father telling of a near fight with a Barra Man who said that all Lochbuie people were thieves, and quoted an old saying as evidence—"Lochbuie, goal of thieves." Father's explanation was that the chief of Lochbuie had a dungeon in which he hid everyone who was in trouble to whom he took a fancy, and so his favor was sought after by anyone pursued by the law or by an enemy. Anyhow, despite the family, I wear a Lochbuie kilt now and then.

6

Two miles east of Seal Cove there was a settlement known as Mull Cove, later known by the inappropriate name of Orangedale. Here were more MacLeods, MacIvers, MacIntyres, MacNeils, MacPhails, Martins, etc. All the people in that area were Presbyterians, as were most of the people in the county of Inverness. On the other hand, the people of the adjoining county of Victoria were mostly Catholics from Skye and Barra—we knew them all as Barra-men. Probably the reformation never reached as far as places like Barra. We were very conscious of the difference between us and the "Barra-men." There was little communication across the county line.

The God of the Presbyterians was, of course, Presbyterian, and his word was the law by which they lived. They live in peace. A lock was so rare that I was half grown before I ever saw one. There were no policemen and no jails or other public service institutions except a madhouse at some distance. The people took care of their own. A Justice of the Peace represented the law of the land, and he was unneeded except when, on rare occasions some cantankerous people got into a dispute. God was the boss as well as the maker of all things. He engineered the universe, and he provided a design for the life of man. One brought up under his sovereignty would never get entirely away from him. The significance he gave to the universe would always make a mere earthbound humanism confining. God might change or fail us, but the awesome majesty of the universe with its power and mystery would remain as would the basic values of his design of life. Paradoxically, these remnants *could* make it difficult for one to remain Presbyterian, because Presbyterianism represented other things in conflict with them.

There was no sentimentalism in this brand of Presbyterianism, nothing suggestive of the evangelism that developed later. A minority of the serious-minded took communion, and such people were expected to represent the righteous life to others. Woe to them when they didn't, for they lost the community's respect. Most good people didn't regard themselves as good enough to be communicants. Nevertheless, all people, including the most flagrantly sinful, were regular church attendants. One might be sinful but one didn't challenge or repudiate God.

Nothing of the loving father came through to me. Really, we had two religions, each with a God: the religion of the soft hearted Jesus and that of the stern Jehovah. And isn't it always necessarily so, this contradiction? One represented the rigid, stern and tragic realities and necessities and the other answered our need as helpless, defenseless creatures whose best hope is the warmth of love. In the Cape Breton of my time, no matter what respect was given Jesus, the Old Testament God was enthroned as the thing that mattered most in all times and places.

I didn't like him. Who could? He disapproved of the very hungers he implanted in us. He watched and recorded every little misstep. He allowed no privacy. That he might forgive never occurred to me. The Devil, on the other hand, was an intriguing puzzle long before I ever formulated a theological problem. At times he was God's enemy; at others, God's tool to keep poor wretches in order. At times he was exciting, like a story character, but he was never as fear-inspiring as God. No one ever seemed to see God, but the appearance of the Devil was reported now and then by those who had imbibed too freely.

Once I overheard a conversation about a neighbor who had encountered His Black Majesty on the long, wooded, lonely Barren Road. After sucking the dregs from his bottle he was swaying back and forth as he followed the road, when a glance behind him revealed the monstrous form of evil catching up with him. There was no doubt about the identity of the thing. The man ran and fell, got up, and ran and ran and ran to the point of exhaustion, but he constantly lost ground. When he finally felt the hot breath of the Evil One on the back of his neck he screamed, and then the creature ran past him. He was big and round as a molasses barrel, with very short legs that somehow did not lessen his speed. Once in front, the apparition burst into a thousand shafts of flame and spluttering stars and disappeared. The man was very ill the next day, retching sorely long after his stomach was empty. That was taken as evidence that he had actually seen the Evil One; no one seemed to connect his vision with his excesses. News of the unseen world was rarely doubted, for in Cape Breton things not of this world held priority over reason.

Cape Breton held the name of God in deep reverence. Rarely was it used profanely. If anyone ever so used it, he did so in English. Yet words like the Devil and hell was excusable. Father used to say, "Abuse the Devil all you like. He deserves it." I remember how when we kids were involved in a first-class squabble, my sister Mary, exasperated almost to the point of violence, came forth with "Jesus H. Christ!" There followed a deathly silence. We had never heard that before, and it shook us. Then mother attended to Mary. The most profane thing about it was the initial.

As time passed and I grew, both the Devil and the Old Testament God tended to give way to the gentle one of Nazareth, a happy substitution that soothed the heart but made a fearful mystery of all the pains and frustrations and tragedies of life.

This suggests something of the spiritual climate in which I grew, and about which I felt keenly at times, long before I could be said to have done any thinking.

SHADOWY WORLD

Someone took me to see the old charred stump underneath which, I was told, they had found me. It was a pleasant revelation. I loved that stump, and later went often to inspect it by myself, just to gaze at it with a glow of wonder and good feeling. I do not recall ever having raised any question about how I had gotten under the stump.

Such recollections are like little pictures imprinted on my mind forever. There are many such. There is always a perfectly steady focus, although I am vaguely aware of other components of the picture. These pictures are of the high points of situations, and generally they lack either beginning or end.

In the first of these pictures, I am standing by a tub in which a woman is washing a scrawny new baby, and she has just asked me if I like the new baby. That is all there is in this picture. If this baby was my youngest brother, Alan, I was just two years and five months old.

At a later time, when I knew something about breeding and begetting among cows and horses, a playmate had just told me that I had originated in exactly the same way as calves and colts. I was deeply shocked, but I think it was the fact of having been deceived, and of Malcolm Hector's pride in

10

superior knowledge that carried the impact. But there the picture is, showing Malcolm so informing me while we watch a couple of men working on a log with a crosscut saw. It is strange how I get into these pictures myself, but I do. In this picture I look embarrassed and crestfallen. I think the embarrassing situations in which my ego suffered are the ones that were most often fixed in my mind, although there are some pictures that were preserved by a high degree of excitement. Most frequently, though, embarrassing moments remain, with a thousand spankings apparently forgiven and forgotten.

Growing from infancy is something like slowly awakening. It takes a long time to dispel the shadows of non-being. It must somewhat parallel the slow emergence of life itself from the sleep of eternity. Life works its way out of sleep and shadow. That's its business.

Although much still existed of a pre-Christian culture deeply rooted in the minds of my people, the culture into which I emerged had everything explained in a Christian way. There was God who put us here in his effort to create something in his own image. The entrance into life, and the exit from it, were known. One just did his best on the way from door to door, while unimaginable things awaited him beyond. Now there is no explanation; I can only wonder. Maybe life is not indigenous to this planet, and came in with astral dirt. If it all started here and nowhere else, the sod takes on a worship-inspiring significance, making Mother Earth a title wisely bestowed upon our planet.

But I am wandering a bit. I was saying that earliest recollections suggest waking, and the answers that first emerged were as puzzling as the shadows. This one, for instance. I am standing tight against the wall at the corner of the house, peeking out at my big brother John, who is going out to chop up kindling for the fire. It is the Sabbath day, and somehow I know that to do work of this sort on this day will be taken seriously by the Eye in the sky. I fully expect John to be struck dead. There is no recollection of how I came by this conviction—from the other kids, probably. This may have been my first great moment of anxiety. No one else seemed concerned, and that troubled me a great deal. John finished his chopping, bundled up the kindling in his arms, went into the kitchen, and started the fire, and nothing at all happened. I was puzzled about God's not acting as I knew he should have.

A very early picture shows me behind the stove in a panic of fear of a white-bearded man who is chasing me around the stove, clicking his bared white teeth, and declaring that he is going to eat me up. There is movement here, but it is caught as in one exposure of a movie film. The family didn't seemed concerned; in fact, they were laughing loudly. Yet I knew that they cared for me very much. I was like the King of Siam, in a puzzlement, and scared stiff as he was not.

I am sitting in a baby's cradle. It is still dark, and Mother, always the first up, is busy preparing and packing Father's lunch by the light of a tall kerosene lamp. The stove is burning briskly and spitting sparks out its front. Father is not in the picture. There is no recollection of how the subject came up, or of its being discussed, but I have just learned that I would die like all other creatures. It was a blow "between wind and water" as a professor of mine at McGill used to say. However, I suspect I survived it before the day was over, for I had, then as now, the only answer to death-life itself. Life came to us in the raw, and there was nothing to sweeten its dire limitations except vitality. It was better that way too, I believe. But there I am in the gloom of an oil lamp, sitting in the cradle, subdued under the weight of my mortality.

Next, I see myself on the ice beyond the open water at the south of the river. The axe I am carrying has gone through the ice to the handle and the water is oozing up. I am carrying a short stick that has a hook and line fastened to one end, going fishing as the grownups did. Anyone on young ice would test it with the axe, and that is what I was doing. But it was a meaningless ritual to me; I didn't know how to identify danger. There was very little ice where I walked, and a strong current underneath. The hazard and the whole picture became fixed in my mind when Mother called from the barn in a fear-laden voice and came running to the shore. I have some vague awareness of being both hugged and spanked, and of hearing

12

for the first time about thin ice and drowning. I was too young to know that death is a hunter whose hunger is never appeased.

I just see my feet in one picture, or perhaps I should say my shoes. They are new and stiff and on the toe of each one is a strip of brass. I am joggled up and down on my mother's knee as she sings—in Gaelic, of course.

"And I will get the brogan, the brogan, the brogan (shoes)
And I will get the brogan, the lovely pointed brogan,
When they come from Oban."

The ditty never meant anything to me until as a Canadian soldier I was on leave in Britain, and found that Oban is the gateway to the Hebrides, and no doubt the marketplace for the outer islands and for much of the south-west region of Scotland. The brass toes suggest that by the time I came along father had given up making shoes for his children, as I know he did for the older ones.

There was a bedroom just off the dining-living room in which guests slept and the ill were cared for. A party of some sort is going on, for there is great laughter and talk. I am standing on the edge of the bed in full view of the company, urinating across the floor. There is one anguished cry, "The oatmeal!" A newly-purchased barrel had been temporarily placed in the room. I am sure that I had been put in that bed temporarily, too. The motivation for my impropriety was the fear of wetting the bed, and I woke up only while the elimination was in process. "Better put a string on him," someone said. Then my mortification was complete, and the picture seared into my mind.

I had been outdoors and in the stables, I suppose. I am standing in the doorway and Father's loud greeting fills the room. "A dhuine Bhec (Little man), there's shit on your shoes." Father knew no synonyms for four letter words. The fixative in this case again was the general laughter—the happiest sound in the world can be one of the cruelest.

Everyone is on his knees with elbow on the seats of chairs, and a strange man with a red beard is talking to the back of his chair in droning candences. That was probably Mr. Rose, the minister, for we never prayed that way except when he called. Prayer was a very personal and secret thing among us and no one ever knew whether or not any of the others prayed. I am sure that all did on occasion, though, for life doesn't let a Celt off without sometimes having to voice the agony and longing of his heart to the Eternal. Our family style of praying, however, was not the approved one; as always, there was a difference between what we approved and what we did.

An old woman—all adults were old then—is sitting on the floor, or rather hanging a bit above it, and a man has the fingers of his right hand in her mouth and has lifted her off the floor. She is poised there for all time. My vague understanding is that the fingers were pressed against the roof of the mouth and that the pressure of her weight was supposed to relieve some pain or other.

I am in bed and Mother and Father are getting ready to retire. I must have been young enough to be sleeping with them. Father is standing naked in the middle of the room. I have no explanation for this memory, unless that was the first time I had seen a grown man undressed. One can justify such a memory without resort to Freud.

Next, I am in bed again, but in the middle of the day and far from sleeping. I had been sent there for misbehaving. I think I had thrown the stove poker at my sister Mary. When we did anything very bad our pants were pulled down and we were properly spanked on our bare buttocks, and in front of everybody. That is what happened to me—the last and most awful humiliation.

There's a series of shots in this one. I am facing Colin and we are both sitting on chairs with our bare feet together, soles to soles. Then I see myself falling head-first through the open cellar trap door. There's the impact on the watery mud in the darkness, and finally I am sitting in a rocker solicitously tended by Mother and my sisters who can't believe that I am not hurt. I wasn't really—didn't feel a scratch or a bruise, but I suspect I was making the most of the situation. I was given a mouthful of watered whiskey. Their concern and attention was wonderful. Colin and I had begun pushing our feet together and he pushed harder and I went over backwards and down, missing three enormous stone steps, and landing in the unfinished part of the floor of hewn logs father was laying. I remember being concerned for the person who had left the trap door open.

There are happy pictures here and there. Colin and I are standing by Uncle Hector's gate, and I have a toy watch in the palm of my hand (it must have been Christmas) which would go when one turned the stem. It had everything but the ability to keep time, but that detracted little from its glowing worth. There's nothing else in the picture.

I am sitting in a chair on the porch gazing in sweet rapture at a smelt, the first fish I ever caught, hanging on a nail high up on the wall out of the cat's reach. I am in a glow of pride and good feeling.

Father is dropping a huge bundle of goods on the floor —shoes for everyone, and a hoselike roll of stocking material that would be cut into proper lengths and have the feet knitted on. I have a sense of my mother's joy over this.

I am gazing intently at the frost forms on the window pane—ferns and trees, and what looks like the image of a man. I have a feeling of having failed to get an answer to some question or other.

Now Father is standing, cap and shoulders covered with snow, with a dead red fox held up in one hand for all to admire. The pleased expression on his face suggests that this was an unusual happening.

My first awareness of men killing each other in wars is filled with anxiety. Father has just returned from work, and is telling of "The States" going to war with Spain. A young man, Neillie John (Ian Ban's son), whom I greatly loved, has just gone to Boston, and I am much concerned about his safety.

15

A neighboring young man has just volunteered for the Boer War. He is walking across the railway bridge on his way to the train that will take him away, and I feel certain that I shall not see him again.

A newspaper shows a Boer soldier wearing a wide-brimmed hat, and I am striking it in anger. I am already a partisan.

I have no recollection of anyone ever speaking of these incidents, and I am quite sure that none of my family share these same memories. They are mine alone, for memory is very personal. They are evidence of my coming into being, with the longings and curiosities and sensitivities of a human. Despite the superior knowledge of modern psychologists, perhaps there is something to William James' characterization of a child's first consciousness as a big booming confusion.

SEAL COVE AND MY PEOPLE

Father slashed a farm out of the wilderness, but he was not a farmer. Before thinking of marriage, he built himself a log cabin. It was roomy and had a basement and a fireplace, but could boast of no other convenience, not even a place in which to bake bread. When Peggy arrived she baked her bread in a contraption he invented which could be buried in the hot coals.

Their marriage would not make any splash in the society columns today, but in its way it was a big affair. There were many people and enough "euste Beha" (water of Life) to make any affair a success. Father used to tell stories about the occasion, such as how citizens along the twelve-mile route from Big Harbour Island to Seal Cove shot off their guns as they passed. At one place someone blew a horn and rang a cow bell, and father regarded this as an unpardonable discourtesy. The marriage service was at Peggy's home, and the "wedding" was in the log cabin at Seal Cove in the evening. All along that rough road "Aonghas Eachen" (Angus Hector) from Valley Mills played the pipes without a halt except at one point where he tried to give the pipes a drink from the bottle. At times he'd miss a note or two when the buggy

17

lurched badly in a hole or struck a boulder. "Aonghas Eachen" was the reason why at first I did not like my own name; he was no great example of propriety, to put it mildly. But Aonghas Eachen's piping that day was considered a great feat. When the procession arrived at Neil's gate, Aonghas got to his feet and whacked the pipes against the gate post, causing them to give forth a last dismal squawk; then he fell out of the buggy. He was too drunk to see the party through, and slept it off in the haystack. Some of the people stayed up until morning, when someone fired two gun shots right by the window of the bride and groom's bedroom. This last was an echo of some ancient custom Father could not explain.

Six children were born in the log cabin, and as they increased in number a railway was built that passed within two hundred yards of the cabin. The railway meant jobs and no immediate insecurity. Father and Uncle Dan built a sawmill on the creek, and so supplied themselves with building material as well as with a promise of a means of livelihood. After the sixth child came, Father built a frame house and a barn, and that is the house in which Alan and Colin and I were born. It is still standing and occupied. I've been told that when I was an infant the house took fire and was almost lost. My sisters used to tell me of how they helped carry me out to safety in the cradle.

The people who settled round about were to be my people, and the soil and water and woods were to be as close and intimate to me as my own soul. Along with God, they set up some severe limitations, but they also provided the values and motives that were to direct me in my transition from the horse-and-buggy days to the space age, and I cannot forget their unparalleled joys. Even the theology of my people saved me from having life begin for me with a burden of mystery.

Locations in the new world were selected without knowledge of their potentiality. Land was cheap and friends were settling in certain areas; those were the lures. Little knowledge was available. What were to be the great productive areas? What markets would open up? What could the soil produce? The properties selected could become the hearts of prosper-

18

ous communities or they could remain wild country outposts destined to decay. The wilderness was most secretive then about its future, and only time could disclose the truth. Yet land and forest and sea and markets determine the character and cultural level of a people. The selection in my grandfather's time was a first-class gamble. The United States, Canada, Australia, South America—what knowledge was available for making a wise selection?

The Scottish Highlanders who came to Cape Breton were not greatly schooled, although many of them were quite literate. But any assets of that sort they may have brought to Cape Breton were soon eliminated by the absence of good institutions of education. And so, many of my father's generation, and mine too for that matter, were practically illiterate. My mother went to school for half a day, but her being the oldest child in her family was enough to indicate that she could not be spared from home duties. My father did a little better, but learned barely enough to read and write when the need for such skills was sufficiently urgent. And that was the way for most people, except a very few like Uncle Dan, who had some high school education. The land and the forest and the sea were the principal teachers, and health and strength and native intelligence were to make trial and error effective enough to meet immediate needs.

Seal Cove should have been named MacLean Cove, for most of the people in the settlement were MacLeans, and they were all at least distantly related, although they came from different parts of the Inner Hebrides. Seal Cove got its name because someone had declared that he had seen a seal there. He probably did see one, for my grandmother MacRae once killed one with an axe.

People built on adjoining properties. Uncle Hector's land adjoined Father's to the east, Uncle Dan's to the north and west. Beyond Uncle Hector, Ian Ban (Blonde Ian) MacLean was located, and beyond him another MacLean and the Monroe family. Across the railway to the south was Donald Og (young Donald), and beyond him were his three brothers, Murdoch, Ian, and Malcolm. All the MacLeans except father and his brothers were known to us as "Banich"—(the light

19

or blond people). Our crowd were known as Collich, the people from Coll. Three or four miles to the west in the deep woods were Donald Nicholson and his family, and near them the MacIntoshes. These two families were so isolated that we thought of them as backwoods people.

The community was not altogther isolated from other settlements. Small business with merchants, and especially the church, bound them to folks at Mull's Cove or Orangedale or at River Deny, Gillis Cove, Valley Mills, and Malagawatch, and somewhat less to the people of Whycocomagh, Big Harbor, and Marble Mountain.

The cove had been formed by the junction of two rivers, and between them there was the neck of land we called Uncle Hector's Point. One branch of the cove came to the foot of Father's property and the other received the stream that emerged from the Monroe property. In this gentle, sheltered cover we had sea water, perhaps diluted a bit by streams in the sixty-odd miles from the entrance to the sea near Sydney. Thus we enjoyed the sea and its life under inland like conditions. Across the mouth of our stream the railway passed on a sizable bridge, providing a slender pathway to other parts of the world and adding much interest and excitement as well as transportation and job opportunities.

The accident of one's place of birth is as significant as blood and family; its demands for survival determine a way of life. A great portion of our diet was sea food, and we acquired a great love for it. The people had to become habituated to boats, fishing, and sailing, as well as to axe and saw. The lake's gentle, briny waters just about ran in our veins. Father's first boat was what he called a log canoe, really a log hollowed out with great labor.

There were other things, too, that had a part in determining our life's orientation. All about us were conifer forests, of which every family had its share. The forests provided fuel and lumber for building, and the coal mines near Sydney would later open up a market for lumber. It was necessary for everyone to acquire skill with tools. The almost self-sustaining farm meant kinship with cows and horses and sheep and all the usual creatures of the farm yard. The soil and marketing conditions were such as would keep people on a low economic level, although the chance to hunt and fish saved them from deprivation. One worked in this theatre of life as soon as he was able to fetch and carry or to lift an axe or hoe or shovel. There were a few specialists— who were called upon when exacting work was required—the carpenter and blacksmith, but mainly the people were their own carpenters and blacksmiths and butchers.

There were some things, however, that were beyond the skill of ordinary untrained folks. No one but the specially trained built a buggy, and there was the clock mender who traveled about now and then. Carriage building was Uncle Hector's trade, and his shop was one of our great delights. People acquired many and varied skills as naturally as they learned to walk. They also acquired a self-sustaining attitude towards life. As soon as anyone could do the work of a man, he was on his own.

There were many shortcomings, some serious ones. Education did not often go beyond the third or fourth grade and was strictly confined to the three rudimentary R's. Our economic status bred in us an inferiority in the presence of any display of wealth, prestige, or unusual learning. Great deference was shown towards the upper class, which was entirely composed of two or three merchants, the doctor, and and minister. Many of my people, under more fortunate circumstances, would have become lawyers, doctors, technicians, and even professors. Some were more highly gifted than some professors I have known; circumstances were less kind than nature.

There were other people I must include, although they did not belong to Seal Cove—knights of the road who traveled about picking up bed and board as they could. Among them were a few who did odd jobs on occasion. There were also the real knights who neither sowed nor spun, but merely walked to the next meal and bed. They belonged to the general area but had no particular abode. There was "Ian Slash" —a MacDonald, I believe—who had a vocational specialty of a seasonal sort. He threshed grain with a hand flail. He was a

21

dimwit, and, to us kids especially, a most amusing personality. I am afraid he did not command our respect. His lack of a chin gave him a fish mouth. Ian Slash had a very special treasure, a dollar watch and chain, which he always displayed. He never wound it, and we welcomed him just for the chance to ask him why he never wound his lovely watch. He would straighten up immediately the question was asked, look at us very seriously, and then tell us that it was very bad for a watch to wind it. That was the high point of his occasional visit. He had been married at one time and had a daughter who was born without a nose. She maintained herself as maid at the Manse, and competently served the minister's family for many years until the day it was discovered that she was in the family way. The rumored identity of the father created a scandal. When she called at our home, Mother would give her buttered bread and tea and maybe fruit if any was available. Afterwards we kids would be on guard against being given the cup she had used. No amount of washing would satisfy us, for we regarded her as repulsively ugly, and the association of the cup with "Nosey", as we called her, was enough. We often cruelly plagued "Nosey". We'd lie in wait for her on the highway and then jump out from the bushes with wild yells and frighten her almost out of her wits. The time came, however, when we understood how unkind such pranks were, and left her in peace. Probably the tanning we received a couple of times helped the development of a conscience.

"Big Charlie" (his last name was MacKinnon) had the reputation of being a scholar, probably because he had had a try at teaching school at one time, and as a consequence a smidgin of the respect in which teachers were held had rubbed off on him. He had a stiff leg and a beard, and quietly pretended to be wise. It was said that once a school teacher who was trying to read a newspaper asked Charlie what the word collision meant. Charlie's reply was that it meant a damn poor school teacher. But Charlie was a bred-in-the-bone bum. He came around frequently about supper time, which meant that he had planned to stay for the night. Quite often he was lousy, and mother kept a special "shakedown" for him that could be laid out on the porch and boiled afterwards.

The name Archie Uthrum (Light Archie) is almost as familiar to me as my own, but I am uncertain as to which of two men it belonged: was he the bearded man who chased me around the stove or was he the alcoholic no-good who came around now and then? I'll dodge the question by calling the latter The Bottle Man for my present purpose. He stirred neither interest nor pity in anyone.

The Bottle Man had a real to-do with my sister Katie. He came, the worse for drink as usual, and was given supper and bed. Katie was grown up enough to feel responsible for some housekeeping duties and got very impatient next morning waiting for the guest to get out of bed. She rapped on his door at nine o'clock, and at ten, eleven and twelve. Then one o'clock passed, and also two o'clock without a word from the guest. By then Katie's ire was thoroughly aroused and she walked into his room with the broom-handle at the ready. She found the man in the act of draining a whiskey bottle and snuggling down for another nap. Katie told him that she was going downstairs for a bucket of water, and if he wasn't up when she returned he would get it all over his head. He was up, all right. She fed him some breakfast and told him the highway was wide open and free for travelers.

At a later time, Donald Cameron, with whom I worked for several summers, told me that once he had found our Bottle Man dead drunk by the side of the road. Like the Good Samaritan he had compassion on the man even though he had not been assaulted by anyone, got him onto his own back, and started off, hoping to find him shelter at the nearest home. That meant carrying him for a mile or more. Donald was both big and strong, but he was tiring fast when he heard a meaningful glug-glug sound, right back of his neck. Looking over his shoulder, he found that his charge was taking a swig from his bottle, probably to help him continue his sleep. "Mac a Dbhoil!" (Son of the Devil!), said Donald. "I picked out the dirtiest part of the ditch I could find and pitched him into it and left him there."

The plague of the road, however, was "Iam Mohr na Ton," (literally, John of the ass). He had once burst his breeches in company. He was always lousy and unbelievably dirty. Mother would never deny anyone food and bed, although the family outvoted her on occasion. She always wept when she saw "Ian Mohr" coming. A shakedown on a bench was not enough to protect people from Ian's pediculous condition. We kids used to stand behind him, or watch his back through a window, just to see the lice crawl. No matter what precautions mother took, she would spend days over the washtub after one of Ian's visits. The lice were the only entertainment he brought us youngsters, and we'd just as soon have done without it.

Then there was "Crazy Tramp", a demented chap who often went the rounds. He carried an axe-handle weighted with a lump of lead, and most people were a bit afraid of him. He was always given food when he called. Wherever he moved, he carried the axe-handle with him and kept it within easy reach of his hand. He was so obviously insane that we were all tense until he left. There came a time finally, when Father buttoned the door in his face and shouted authoritatively, "No admittance!" After pounding on the door again he left, loudly grumbling and brandishing his club.

There was a place at Mabou where the violently insane were incarcerated. The feeble-minded, and sometimes these violently insane, were cared for by their families, but the dimwits were not easily contained, and were allowed to wander.

I should not overlook a class of people who brought us no end of fun and so often broke the monotony of life for us. Conspicuous among them were the peddlers, men who trod the roads carrying enormous loads of goods on their backs. They made up somewhat for there being no Fifth Avenue where people could window-shop. They were of various Mediterranean stocks and were great salesmen; they would spread their goods out on the floor to entice any of us who had pennies to spend. They were alien enough in appearance and speech to be most interesting, and they ranged in age from the early teens to the fifties. We asked one black-bearded man where he came from, and he told us he came from Jerusalem. My brother Duncan, who must have been about fourteen years old at the time and who had very little knowledge of geography or theology, said in incredulous amazement, "You

24

mean you came from Heaven above?" These men were always given food and bed according to their need, and they always gave Mother something—a bar of scented soap, a comb, or a package of pins.

There were many men who traveled through on foot just once and who needed food and shelter; they came in groups as well as singly. They generally followed the railway, and many of them were sailors who had jumped ship at Sydney and set out on foot to the Strait of Canso, where they hoped to find a berth on another ship. Once six fine Swedes came, who seemed to be embarrassed because they spoke such poor English—they didn't know that ours was about as bad. When they left they filled Father's pockets with fine stringy tobacco for his pipe. That was all they had to give along with their much-appreciated courtesy.

There were two sailors whose names I happen to remember, who impressed us very favorably. After they told us a lot of tall tales we discovered that the one whose name was Kennedy was a violinist, and brother Neil had a fiddle. We were wonderfully entertained that night. Kennedy played and Schofield danced. The dancer nearly brought the house down when he did a sailor's hornpipe, for he was a big man and wore an enormous pair of hobnailed boots. Luckily we had no carpets. My family greatly enjoyed dancing, although it was not much approved of by the church leaders.

There were some psychotics among the wayfarers, and also some common types. One came as a cattle buyer and said he would buy all the cows that would pass his inspection. The man wore a white shirt and looked like a gentleman. He went over our herd and expressed great satisfaction, suggesting flattering prices for a number of the animals. Father was for selling the whole lot to him, but mother reminded him that since he never raised a hand to tend the cattle and couldn't tell how many he had in the herd, she was having a say in the selling if there was to be any selling. Nevertheless most of the cattle were eventually marked for sale. The buyer stayed with us and occupied the guest room at night while in the daytime he inspected all the cattle in the community, and many of them were tagged for sale. People were extremely excited—

we'd all be rich! This went on for nearly two weeks, and then the man left with a long list of animals that, he said, would be sent for immediately; he would arrange with the railway for transportation and let people know when to ship. He would pay freight too. Of course we never heard from him again.

There was a man who claimed that Alexander Graham Bell had stolen his invention of the telephone from him. I felt enraged at this theft, but a bit nonplused when my brother John cast doubt on the whole story. "He must be crazy," he said, 'Didn't you notice how he would stop talking and started mumbling to himself? He's a looney." The disclosure disappointed me.

There was also the dashing, garrulous fellow who told us of the great apple orchards in the Grand Pré country where he owned several orchards, and promised to send us barrels of apples that would otherwise be wasted. He said he produced hundreds of barrels a year but couldn't market all he grew. We had him tagged at once for what he was.

We had two Negro families at nearby Marble Mountain. They had been brought up with the Highland folks, and Gaelic was their native tongue. Their English was as faulty as ours. We never thought of these families as different. They were exciting people. The two fathers loved debates, of which there were many, and these two men, who were brothers, were always opposing each other. I remember one such debate, which was on the question of peace or war as agents of social progress. One of the men was all for peace; he spoke eloquently and made quite a speech. Then his brother countered with the statement: "If my good brother had had peace all the time, he would still be hoeing cotton in the deep South."

Then one day the railway brought us another and different Negro. He was a giant of a man, and athletic. He spoke flowery English and was a gifted story teller. From him I first learned of the slave trade. His father had been a slave who ran away and worked his way north. When invited to supper, this guest said he had no need of food, but would enjoy a glass of milk. He said he had asked the cow down by the creek for some, but he guessed that she spoke only Gaelic. I loved this man intensely, and was grieved to see him go.

Mother's cupboard was often bare because of these transients, but we small fry learned a great deal from them, and they added much excitement to our lives. On rare occasions there would be some who had to be invited to leave, a most embarrassing business. After Ian Ban died and his boys had left, his home was vacant. One evening three men took it over and stayed in it several days. Widow Mary MacNeil, a cousin of ours, lived at the next place beyond Ian Ban's, and the strangers pestered her with repeated demands for food and frightened her two young children. They roamed about at night and were very noisy. My brother John had a job at the time, and when he left for work one morning he said he would roust the "buggers" out when he came home. Enough was enough, and it was time these fellows were invited to take to the road again. But we had a guest, a neighbor whom we called "Begod" because he so often used the phrase. He was really Neillie Malcolm, a nephew of Donald Og's. Begod heard John say his piece, and said he could build a fire under the "bastards" himself. He took John's new breechloading shotgun from the wall, shoved a couple of shells into it, put a couple more in his pocket, and invited us kids to go along with him and see the fun. Mother protested, but we were thrilled. Before we left, someone said the tramps had moved to Uncle Hector's old vacant place, and so we headed for that direction. Begod pounded on the door and shouted, "Money, or your life! I mean come out with your hands up." We got a giggle out of that. No one responded to repeated poundings, and so we concluded that we had been misinformed and went on to Ian Ban's. When we approached the house we stood still and Begod shouted, "Hey, you fellows in there! It's time you hit the road." Nothing happened. Begod walked up close to the door, raised the gun heavenwards, fired both barrels, and reloaded. Then he shouted, "The next time I shoot I'll be blasting your asses with buckshot. Come out with your hands up, and come running, and I mean running." They came. The first two were running, but the third walked slowly with a cynical smirk on his face. Begod aimed the gun at him, and he also ran. We followed them down the road a way to make sure they did not return. He had always regarded Begod as a kittenish sort of fellow, but now we were thrilled to find he had more guts than most.

In a sense, all these people should be numbered among my people, for they belonged to our time and place even though they were mostly transient. What more can one's people do than enrich one's memory?

SOMETIMES THERE WAS A SCHOOL

I have an old snapshot of the first school I attended. It was a little twenty-by-thirty foot building set in a small, stump-filled opening in the woods close by the rutty, muddy horse-and-buggy road. The front end of the school attic had a diamond-shaped window, which was the school's most distinctive feature. There was a lobby for outer clothing when some of us were lucky enough to own outer clothing; most of us had nothing more than a cap and mittens to deposit there. Inside the building were two rows of eight-foot, home-made desks, each with a backless plank bench. There were more benches at the back along the wall, which were rarely used except for boys who slid slyly along them to get near the door before dismissal time. At the front of the room there was a raised platform with the teacher's desk on it. Back of that there hung a pine blackboard. The cracks between the boards seemed to be designed for breaking chalk. There were two maps, one on each side of the blackboard. One pictured Nova Scotia, with the counties clearly marked; the other was a map of the world showing both hemispheres. One corner was torn, and drooped. The map was rarely if ever used.

29

I was eight years old the first time I attended school. Why so late? Probably because we had been some years without school, or maybe because I didn't have good enough clothes. It was a sunny winter's day, and the walk to school was most interesting. A bridge crossed our stream just at Uncle Dan's gate, and I was rushed across it by my sisters because, they said, some kind of monster was under it which would get me if I didn't run. The snow was deep and fresh and white, and it sparkled in the intense light like jewels. Here and there we inspected body prints left by other children. They had thrown themselves on their backs and raised and lowered their arms to leave impressions like winged angels. An almost invisible snowshoe hare bobbed along in front of us for a spell. When we got to where the road was heavily bordered on each side by woods, the air was still, and all about us was hushed with a sense of mystery.

When just in sight of the schoolhouse we crossed a little bridge over the waters of two brooks that had just found each other and would keep together on their journey to the sea. One came from right behind the school, and the other, the one that brought us our drinking water, from deep in the woods.

The school was cold that day, and the children were huddled about a rectangular stove in the center of the room. The fathers brought the firewood to the school, but the bigger boys had to prepare it for the stove. This time the boys had been negligent, and the wood was green, and wet with sap. It sizzled in the stove and gave off little heat. The teacher was not in the least perturbed; no doubt she was used to it.

Every class stood up in a row in the center of the floor, one after the other, and read. At the end of each reading lesson there were words listed for spelling, and children were tested on them. When one failed a word the next one tried, and if he succeeded he moved up ahead of the one who had failed. Sometimes the one at the very bottom moved to the top of the class in a glow of triumph. Once at the top, it was a matter of pride to retain first place. When all had read, the teacher took me up to stand beside her at her desk, and with her arm around me, started me on the Primer. It was a dog-eared, hand-me down copy. On the first page was the alphabet in capitals, and on the next the alphabet in small letters. The unfamiliarity of the English language was a difficulty, but in a few days I mastered the alphabet and began spelling out the words. At the top of the first reading page were small pictures of a dog, a cat, a hen, a pig, a tub, and a fly, the appropriate word under each picture. I took school work very seriously rushing home every day to report progress. This was the beginning of a long journey for me. If when I left school that first day someone had told me that I would be in school as a student and teacher for the rest of my active life I might have made an end of it right there. Of course it was not possible even for a lively imagination at that time to conceive of such a future. Only a very few got as far as high school studies, and most of those did not get beyond the first or second year.

The routine of the school was soon to become very familiar to me. The first thing in the morning we did our reading lessons, and then dug into arithmetic until recess time. After recess came more arithmetic, except for a few older students who studied a health reader that had mostly to do with anatomy. One black figure showed the nervous system in white, another showed the muscles, and so on. At noon we went home for lunch, fun, and fights on the way. We brought lunches to school only when the weather was very bad. Right after lunch we practiced writing in a copy-book, copying sayings like "Honesty is the best policy," "A stitch in time saves nine," "Anno domini, in the year of our Lord, anno Domini," and such sayings. Then we had more arithmetic, and on some afternoons some classes in geography. Geography meant memorizing the counties of Nova Scotia. Why this was so important was and is a mystery to me. We recited those counties so much that they were more familiar to us than the multiplication tables or the Lord's prayer: Inverness, Victoria, Cape Breton, Richmond, Guysborough, Halifax, Lunenburg, Queens, Shelburne, Yarmouth, Digby, Annapolis, Kings, Hants, Cumberland, Colchester, Pictou, and Antigonish. To get through to Antigonish without a mistake was a triumph. I still get a sense of accomplishment when I say Antigonish.

Sometimes there was recess in the afternoon if the teachers preferred it to getting through the day ten minutes or so earlier. The last thing we did on Fridays was to recite bits of poetry. The ambitious ones would memorize reams of poetry, but most of the boys would pick out the shortest and easiest things they could find in their schoolbooks. Sometimes we fought over who should have the privilege of reciting

> Love not to talk
> Love not to boast,
> Grief comes to him
> Who brags the most.

There were other moralistic gems such as

> 'Tis wilful waste brings woeful want
> And I may live to say,
> Oh how I wish I had the crust
> Which once I threw away.
>> Whene'er a task is set to you,
>> Don't idly sit and view it,
>> Nor be content to wish it done,
>> Begin at once and do it.

The teacher never appreciated such bits of poesy, for they identified the lazy ones.

One bit of fun was the occasional spelling bee that was at times substituted for the recitations. We were lined up in a long row from the front to the back of the room. When one failed to spell a word, he or she had to sit down. A number of boys always went down on the first try, and I was often among them. The undefeated one was either king or queen. It was usually queen, and she was usually either Flossy Murdoch or Margaret Dan.

Once I recall seeing a big book on the teacher's desk. It was open and had lovely colored pictures of grasses and flowers and grains. It was probably resource material sent from the province's office of education, but such things were never used and were rarely available. The teachers should not be judged too harshly, for they were mostly poorly prepared and, anyhow, the prescribed books had to be covered.

We had one or two good teachers, such as Mary Mac-Leod, who was a natural student and a gracious person. There was another who seemed to know something, but I never liked her; I think that was because of what she did to Alan. He was trying to split wood right after a pouring rain. He was wearing his Sunday suit, which someone had sent him from Boston, and when he splashed mud on it he said "Damn!" One of the girls at once told the teacher and so, after recess, Alan was stood up before her and she took a birch switch to him. He held out his hands as she commanded, and took the switching without wincing. She was unhappy about this and kept on switching him in an effort to make him cry. Calm and unperturbed, he looked her in the eye as though he had some studious interest in what she was doing. When she gave up she had made at least one enemy for life, and it wasn't Alan. Almost all our teachers were kind and terribly in earnest, but as unlucky in their education as the rest of us. I don't believe we ever had one in that school who had finished high school.

Teachers were generally given board and room in a series of homes: two weeks with us, two with Uncle Dan's family, two with Donald Og's, and so on. They were paid little more, if any, than a hundred dollars a year.

One thing about the curriculum surprises me now that I look back on it, and that is the meagre use made of the Bible. It wasn't even read except very rarely. Teachers were not highly versed in Biblical education, and probably the school was not regarded as the place where religious teaching should be given emphasis.

What we did at recess time, if done today, might very well be called "creative recreation". Amusement and play were things one sought for himself. The idea of hiring anyone to help children play would have been an earth-quaking joke. We played as the seasons and the surroundings suggested. Snow, hills, and ice in winter, and the stream and lakes and quiet woods with their wild life were more than adequate from a child's point of view. We had the greatest of recreation directors, the unspoiled out-of-doors. Spring brought its excitements—ice breaking up, floods, the birth of all farm animals, and flowers such as the trailing arbutus; and summer brought wild fruit. For some reason the railway embankments produced crops of strawberries and old burnt lands offered abundance of raspberries, while any old pasture produced bunchberries when they were in season, crunching and eating even the seeds. In fact we ate almost anything that would not poison us. As for games, we favored a game of tag which we played on the roadway. One person would be selected to stand in the middle of the road, and he would try to catch the others as they ran past him from one side to the other. Each one he caught joined him as catcher until everyone was on the road. There was no danger from traffic, since there were barely more than two or three horse-drawn vehicles in a day. Donald Nicholson's daughter came home from Boston with her children a couple of times for long enough periods for the children to attend school. They introduced fancy new games like "lazy Betsy" and "in and out the window." These were singing games, and they were very popular with the girls. The boys thought they were sissy, especially the one that said, "kneel down and kiss your lover," and that kind of stuff.

There were the brooks which were easily damned to provide power for home-made paddle-wheels. And what greater delight is there for youngsters than sailing boats down a roaring brook after a heavy shower? The curriculum might have been narrow, but the recreation was as broad as heaven and earth.

There was one fun-producing preoccupation that I look back on with a chill. The railroad crossed the highway less than a hundred yards from the school, and jets and spaceships of today provide less of a thrill than did those trains. When a train whistle was heard at recess or at noon hour we would rush to the crossing to have a closer look, and I mean close. A great game was to put pins and nails and bits of wire on the rails and have them flattened into curious shapes by the weight of the trains. It was fun too to initiate the younger kids into laying an ear on the rail to listen to the clicking noises of an approaching train still not in sight. On each side of the crossing there was a "cattle guard" eight or nine feet square and four feet deep over which the rails were carried on heavy beams. These pits were tempting. Flossie Murdoch once stayed in one of them while a long freight train passed over her. She came out scared to death and with a blob of oil on the top of her head, but what had really frightened her was finding a big black snake down there with her. The bigger boys often grabbed a stake pocket on a flatcar and hung there for a hundred yards or so.

The time came, however, when news of our doing got to the railway authorities, and things began to happen. One day we were astonished by a couple of trainmen who stood in the coal hopper back of the engine and threw lumps of coal at us. I honestly believe they tried to hit us, and some of the lumps they threw were big enough to do serious injury. After that happened several times we learned to keep our distance until the coal hopper passed us.

Then the real scare came. A train stopped one day while school was in session and dropped off a man in uniform—blue cloth with gold braid here and there, and a cap with a lot of golden spinach. He came right to the school, walked in, and took over. He warned us about playing with trains. "There's a penitentiary in New Brunswick for people like you," he said. That produced chills. Then he told us that someone had put a lot of scrap iron on the rails about a mile west of the crossing and had come very close to derailing a train; he was angry and accused us of the crime. One of us had done it, he declared, and he was going to find out which. We had never seen a policeman before, and no policeman ever appeared afterwards at Seal Cove. None of us had ever gone as far as a mile west of the crossing except the MacIntosh children, Malcolm and Amy. The policeman soon found that out and gave all his attention to them. Amy was so frightened that she was speechless, but Malcolm pleaded innocent. He was cruelly quizzed and threatened, and was told he might as well confess because it was obvious that he had done it. But Malcolm kept saying "No", until we were all convinced that he was telling the truth. Although the officer was still convinced that he had found the culprit, he had to give up. And that is how the fun went out of playing with trains.

The decorum at school was less than perfect, and we needed constant surveillance. It was such a temptation to fill our slates with funny pictures and pass them to our friends, to throw things, and to chew spruce gum, which the teachers gathered up periodically and threw into the stove; we often retrieved it and blew off the ashes. We plagued the teachers with requests to go out, and as soon as one of us returned a dozen hands would be up pleading, "Please may I go out?" To say no to all such requests might prove embarrassing to all of us. There were no toilets except the woods. I once heard a teacher talking to Father about this situation. He replied in Gaelic, "Gillie rean lechd be's e tric a cak, agus heth e fatha les." Politely translated, that meant, "A stringy, lazy boy will often want to go, and he'll go a long way with it."

Taylor MacDonald at Orangedale used to sell a fizzy kind of drink that came in bottles with a permanent spring cork. We had lots of these bottles, and when one of us went to the brook for a drink he generally came back with several bottles of water which he gave out to reaching hands. For some reason we were allowed to indulge in drinking water during school hours.

As time for dismissal approached, many boys would slide along the benches at the back an inch at a time until they were close to the door when the happy moment came. We also, surreptitiously, swapped seats, which greatly annoyed teachers.

There were moments of greatly prized excitement. Once the school filled up with smoke, and we discovered that there was a fire in the attic. What fun to have something like that happen, for which no one was to blame! The only access to the attic was a small hatch. There was no ladder, but some of us shinnied up the wall, and others ran for water. Soon pails were sent up on some kind of improvised rope, and we doused the fire thoroughly. The room below was flooded and school was dismissed for the day.

The school had practically no equipment except the two maps. There was no globe, and no books except authorized readers and arithmetic books. There was one teacher who indulged us with a story now and then in the late afternoons,

36

but I was in graduate school at Columbia before I discovered the bonanza of children's books, and caught up on fairy tales. Once the school prescribed Dicken's "A Christmas Carol" for the upper grades, and one of the mothers declared it a lot of .ies and threw it into the stove. I remember a teacher who gave my sister Flora a storybook as a prize for exceptional progress. That and a farmer's book I once received with a newspaper subscription were all the books besides school books that I remember in my home—the Bible excepted of course, because that was the word of God, not just a book.

At times a teacher could not be found, and those children who were old enough to go to Orangedale in winter weather went to school there. My first experience at that school is memorable. Johnnie Brec (speckled or freckled Johnnie), a tough kid of my own age, was a menace to all he could pester. His reputation was worse than he actually was, or rather it did him more credit as a fighter than he deserved. Sometime before this first day at school I was allowed to go to the store at Orangedale by myself, and I met Johnnie at the railway station. I had lived in such fear of meeting him that I was unable even to try to defend myself. He searched my pockets and appropriated all the candy that Merchant Dan had given me, and my jackknife as well. I was humiliated, and tried without success to keep the meeting a secret.

And so I approached the Orangedale school that first day with no little apprehension. The minute I entered the door Johnnie Brec came from behind it, and grabbing me by the throat, began to shove me back and forth. It gave me some courage to be able to remove his hands from my throat; otherwise I evaded him. At the lunch hour, during which we ate bread and molasses sandwiches and drank cold tea, Johnnie attacked my cousin and special friend Duncan Dan, who was two years younger than Johnnie and I. He shoved him about and then knocked him down. I couldn't stand seeing Duncan Dan abused. I took on the Orangedale terror, and with fists flying we fought up and down the aisles of the schoolroom. I finally backed him into the lobby where the walls had not been finished, and the shingle nails stuck through. I pummeled him against the wall, and when he began to bleed from the nails he quit cold, and declared to all onlookers that I was his

37

special friend and that we two could lick the whole school. Colin and Alan also had to beat him before he called them friends. Alan was a real surprise to him. Although younger, he was bigger than Johnnie, and he finished him off by picking him up by the ankles and pounding his head on the ground.

The Orangedale school was a great improvement on my home school. The desks and seats were factory-made. The blackboard was twice as large, there were more maps, and the globe was a wonder to behold. There were still no books except "schoolbooks" in the narrow sense. The room was bigger and housed more children. It was heated by a tall, pot-bellied stove for which we did not have to chop wood, for it burned coal. The boys took turns getting to school early to start the fire, and we kids who had two miles to walk were not excepted. The coal was dumped outside, and in winter it took no little labor to dig it out of the snow and ice. It was soft coal that froze like mud.

The curriculum was substantially the same, but better administered. On the whole, we had more good teachers than poor ones. Margaret MacRae was outstanding, and a man by the name of MacLean who was no relation of ours was a college graduate and a superb teacher. He chewed tobacco and used the coal scuttle frequently. He was a kindly man who delighted us with his sly sense of humor.

There was one real crumb, and perhaps Freud could explain why I have forgotten her name. She used the strap freely until Johnnie Brec, taking advantage of her absence at noon hour, cut the strap up into little squares and left them in a neat pile in the middle of her desk. She suspected me, but had no evidence to justify a whaling. But she got to me eventually. One day Kenny Murdoch filled a sheet of paper with dirty pictures and, reaching from behind me, put his artistic effort on my desk. Just then Miss Blank pounced. She lambasted my hands with a stout pointer until they were red and lumpy. There was nothing to do but beat the devil out of Kenny on the way home, which I did with malice aforethought and no subsequent regrets.

At the beginning of the new term I found myself so much bigger than the other kids that I skipped from fifth grade to first-year high school; no one paid any attention to my taking this liberty. The new teacher was a willowy, giggling person whom I disliked on sight. One day while I was doing a geometry exercise on the blackboard she suddenly started giggling and the kids joined her. I suspected that my shirttail was out or something of the sort, and when I felt behind to make sure, the whole school went into fits of laughter. The teacher was by this time in the grip of hysterical laughter. The game went on, until overcome with anger, I hurled the pointer at the blackboard as hard as I could and went to my seat. She kept me after school and began lecturing me about giving the young children such a bad example. I told her that in my judgment she had given a worse one. I was angry and for good cause, but she had been discourteous without cause, and I walked out and never went back.

I got an opportunity to go to Little Harbor and live with a kind and gracious MacGregor family while attending school. On weekends I walked ten or twelve miles home and back again. In winter I shortened the road a bit by crossing on the ice from Malagawatch. The teacher at this school was a high school graduate and, as such, a qualified teacher, but unfortunately she had no skill in keeping order. A hubbub of some sort was going on most of the time, and serious study was almost impossible. I am afraid I didn't help the poor woman very much as I might have—indeed, I initiated disorder at times. Once I asked to go outdoors, and on the way back I saw that a pane was missing in the attic window. Picking up a pebble I threw it, and by good luck it went through the open pane and bounced along the attic floor, to the great delight of the children below. When I went back in, Archie MacRae, a cousin of mine, asked in a stage-whisper if I had thrown something in, and I winked at him. He immediately went out, and in less than a minute there was a tremendous crash and the noise of splintering glass. He had thrown a sizeable rock, and either his aim or his luck wasn't as good as mine. He struck the center of the sash and the whole window caved in. Everyone had a delightful time.

On another occasion I brought a dart I had made from a cork, a feather, and a horseshoe nail. When a disturbance broke out between two kids and they started throwing ink at each other, I threw the dart at the ceiling, where it stuck with an arresting thud. Next day kids came with pockets filled with darts, and in a few minutes the ceiling was speckled with them. The poor teacher was frantic. She tried to sweep them down, and one stuck in the top of her head. More fun, in which I didn't share. I was really ashamed of myself. I learned very little that year.

Stung by the loss of a year which I could not afford, I set out to look for a school that would allow me to pursue high school studies. To my knowledge there was only one high school in the county, all of thirty miles from my home, and so it would be necessary to have high school instruction from an elementary school teacher. This privilege was more than most school trustees were willing to give to outsiders; a high school student would take too much of a teacher's time and attention, they said.

So my journeys to Valley Mills, Malagawatch, and Marble Mountain were of no avail. The Marble Mountain people were courteous but firm in their refusal. The Malagawatch school I was glad to pass up, for the teacher there knew less than I did. I made two visits to the chairman of the board of trustees at Valley Mills. The first time he quizzed me about my family and neighbors until I was wrung dry of news and gossip. Then he asked me to come again. I returned a couple of days later, and met him in a hayfield. He sat against a stack and hemmed and hawed when not questioning me about my ambitions. Finally he stood up and threw away the wisp of hay he had been chewing, and told me the trustees had said no.

I was in a deep state of depression when I reached home. I went into the house and took my heavily-ladden book bag and threw it over the woodpile, saying that I could get along like the other members of the family. Mother cried, saying over and over that she had had hopes. I hadn't gotten over my pout before Father came home and told me that I should see

Dan Martin, one of our Orangedale merchants. He had said that there was a minister at North Sydney who wanted a schoolboy who could tend his fires and his guests' horses.

And so it happened that I had one good year in an excellent city school, which made all the difference in the world to me. The minister was Dr. T. Chalmers Jack, who was in many ways superior to most ministers. He was a profound student of history and a linguist. His Greek and Hebrew were as good as his English, which was superb. Can anyone ever get over his first encounter with a real scholar and gentleman? My experience with this man's family and the school opened a way out of the maze of circumstances that imprisoned and wasted so many good minds and spirits.

There was another factor involved in my education besides hard work and opportunity—I may have been one of the last humans to become an offering unto the Lord. Originally, I was to have been named Alan when christened, but as it turned out I was named Angus after the minister who did the christening. For a time, as I grew, I wasn't sure if I was who I was supposed to be, but I had extra motivation—indeed, a fixed sense of destiny. God had put his finger on me; that was the way things had been arranged. My Uncle Colin MacRae always called me "Reverend," and everyone seemed to know my destiny, or at least its direction. I am sure that if it hadn't been for God's interference, the fourth grade would have stopped me as it did so many.

I was a happy child, and have always been happy about my childhood and my people. My one deep regret is that I didn't have a teacher who could read the out-of-doors for me. I had a deep and somewhat incommunicable readiness for the wonders of life about me, but, unfortunately, trees remained just trees and rocks, and my wonderings about sky and winds and ice and snow remained unnurtured and enlightened. But I had motivation, and a slit of light did break through the dark barriers of circumstance.

AND ALWAYS THERE WAS CHURCH

No one in the family undertook to teach religion to us younger ones, but we were sent to the Orangedale Sunday School when we were old enough. What we had had there in the way of teaching was an elaboration of what we already knew without being formally taught—God's sovereignty, the Devil and hell, and that one must not steal, kill another human being, commit adultery, bear false witness, be dishonest, tell lies, or be greedy and covetous; that one must be honorable, kind, just, speak the truth courageously, study the Bible, go to church, and keep the Sabbath in holy idleness. There was an ethical core there that became my core. Time was to change my ideas about God, the Devil, the Bible, and the Sabbath, but integrity, honesty, truth-telling and the overwhelming sense of the sovereignty of whatever made and governed life, no matter how named, were in my guts as well as in my mind, and not to be ousted. But I was wide open to knowledge and thought, and so my faith was open to some refinement. In the day-to-day routine little was said about religion, yet we were deeply religious without being pious. There were some who were pious in the better, and some in the worst sense of the word, and they played a significant role: the sincerely upright won respect, while those who lived a pretense were subject to scorn and ridicule.

42

Father wasn't a praying man, but he knew a nice grace to say at table and said it at times when the guests were the praying sort. We regarded that as a weakness, while being a bit overawed by the beauty of the prayer. There was a general regard and reverence for God and his word, although no one was given to gabbing about the faith. Perhaps Hoot MacKenzie, who was supposed to be simpleminded, said it as well as I could now. The Minister, Mr. Rose, met him on the road one day and pulled up his horse to pass the time of day. Hoot at once asked him bluntly, "Where are you going?" "Oh", said Mr. Rose, "I am looking for the lost sheep of the house of Israel." "Foolish to do that," Hoot replied. "I used to waste time looking for them that way, but now I let them go until the winter winds drive them home." So it was with my family. God was in charge of things, and one had better keep that in mind.

It was somewhat different on the Sabbath. Everyone went to church and listened to the minister, who carried the authority of scholarship and of unusual familiarity with the Bible. But his words were not accepted on his authority alone; the word had to be reasonable as well as scriptural, and so religion was discussed on the way home from church and after church in homes to which people might go for a "ceilidh" or visit. My home was a favorite gathering-place. The main church was at Malagawatch, but there was a hall at Orangedale, really a subsidiary preaching station, where services were held in midweek as well as on some Sundays. After some of these evening services men often gathered at our home. They would come in, lower the wicks in their lanterns, set them on the floor near the kitchen door, and select a place where they could tilt their chairs against the wall, fill their pipes, and settle down for a chat. There was no expressed intention of discussing religion, but, with the service fresh in their minds, such discussion ensued as a matter of course. They spoke freely, and there was never any suggestion that anyone was speaking a heresy. One might be wrong, but he was never heretical—my people didn't even know the word. Peter Nicholson, old Donald's only son, was always present, and very often the discussion centered on his strange views. Colin and Alan and I were usually lying half under the stove

43

on the floor with the dogs, Dixy and Purdy, and listening intently. We thought Peter was batty, although he was closer to classic Presbyterianism than any of them. He was an extreme determinist: God had everything planned for us, and nothing but what happened could happen; whatever would be would be. He was often ridiculed for this, and especially for his view that good men might go to Hell and some unworthy ones to Heaven. Our people were too low on the educational-economic scale to be aware of, or concerned about, credal requirements. Freedom on the lower social levels has been too little noted. On occasion, even the Bible might be questioned, even though interpretation could not be doubted. My brother Neil, by then a teen-ager who did his own thinking, once joined in the discussion. The minister had preached on the tree that bore no fruit and was consequently withered with a curse. This story really stopped most of them because they could not accept it as true, and yet there it was in the Bible. It presented no problem to Peter; the tree was blasted as the Bible said. Young Neil's comment stuck in my mind. It was, "I don't believe he ever did it, and if he did, it was a fool thing to do. Father tried to cover up for him by suggesting that perhaps "tree" didn't really mean a tree. It was a lame effort, but good enough to allow the discussion to proceed.

The church at Melagawatch seemed enormous to me, and it was generally filled. The only color in the place was the scarlet velvet and the two enormous tassels that hung from the top of the pulpit. The windows were very tall but had no stained glass. Our family had a pew well towards the back which wasn't quite enough to accommodate us all. It was made of bare, painted pine boards, and the seats were at a precise right angle and without cushions of any sort. We crowded into this seat and listened to two services, one in Gaelic and one in English. We kids did not listen much to the sermons although we liked the fiery preaching as everyone did, but we had a consuming interest in what went on. The collection plate with its burden of copper was always interesting. Once I saw Lauchie Donald put a nickel on the plate and then pick off four pennies. That would bring a laugh almost anywhere.

"Green Malcolm" (our private name for him) had a singing voice that would disturb a salamander. He had always wanted to be a precentor. There were usually two to four precentors, and, of course, no organ. Once in a while a precentor would use a tuning fork, but this accessory was rarely used. One day all but one of the regular precentors was absent, and "Green Malcolm" got his chance. In the Gaelic service the psalms were chanted. The precentor would read-sing a passage, and then the whole congregation would chant the same words, dragging them out to great lengths. Malcolm selected an easy one, the twenty-third. He gave out bravely with, "The Lord's my sheperd, I shall not want," and then piped up for the chant but went away off key. He tried again, but with the same result. After failing a third time he said, as if talking to himself, "Can't do it, Malcolm," and tried again, and then the other precentor took over, and the people sang in quavering voices. The embarrassing moment was over. I thought of the time I tried to recite at school and couldn't recall a single word. Sometimes the chant gripped me with its pathos and I found it deeply moving. The pains and tribulations of Isreal were known to these people from experience.

When there was communion the "sheep" were seated in the center between the two aisles and the "goats" in the outer sections. Perhaps I can suggest the nature of such occasions by relating my own experience at my first communion, although my experience was certainly not like that of the typical communicant. I was very young to take such a step. Duncan Dan first made the suggestion; it would be considered appropriate, he thought, because of our aspirations for the ministry. Duncan and I were separated in the seating procedure. I was given a token at the door—a rectangular bit of white metal which would be collected later to make sure that no unauthorized person sat at the Lord's table. After some instruction from an aged elder the service began. A visiting minister gave the sermon, and I remember it for good reason. He told us of the love of God, a doctrine not then very familiar to me, of his willingness to forgive, and of his power to cleanse away our sins. "Though your sins be as scarlet they shall be as wool," he assured us. It was a warm invitation. Then came the "elements", passed around by the elders with great dignity and solemnity. When the bread came to me I had the world's worst time trying to control a giggling fit, which then and later worked woe with my conscience. There was nothing irreverent about it—it was a reaction to tremendous tension. Somehow I had thought that the "sacred bread" would be some uniquely fancy kind of bread, but when it came it looked just like a plate of mother's bread broken up for the chickens. I was sure that the Devil himself had put such a comparison into my mind, and I told him to get behind me. I've been through a war and in some other tight places, but never in any situation as terrible as that one. Then the wine was passed in a tall silver goblet, and everyone took a modest sip. Anyone who raised his head and tossed it back would be noted. The goblet was passed from person to person. The man who passed it to me had wine dripping from his moustache, but I was composed now, and the Devil worsted. Then a cork popped loudly up front. The elders had underestimated the amount of grape juice needed, and perhaps some of it had fermented. Brother Duncan said later that he would bet the old boys had something stronger than juice. But that was in any case a completely isolated incident. The service resumed and we had another sermon, or maybe it was the last part of one sermon, although it seemed to have no kinship with the previous discourse. Its burden was the eternal damnation that awaited those who ate and drank at the Lord's table unworthily, who "ate and drank damnation unto themselves." I was deeply offended, not so much by the teaching as by the method employed. It all sounded to me like, "Now you're hooked; you are going to catch hell if you don't toe the mark." It was about then that I looked across the church and spied my father and mother among the "goats." Most people did not think themselves good enough to take communion, and I knew Father and Mother thought so. What was I doing? Telling the world that I thought myself better than they or declaring an intention to be as decent as I could be? I was in a sad and baffled state of mind. But no one else seemed to see anything out of the way in the situation, least of all my parents, and so I stopped worrying about it.

But most of my thought is with the years before this event. I have already suggested the serious dignity with which religious affairs were carried out, and my earliest recollections do not bring me anything suggestive of evangelism; my experience with that did not begin until quite late in my elementary school years. But change is inevitable, and one night at an Orangedale service an evangelist did the preaching. Billy McNab, as I shall call him, was reared somewhere in the general area. Then he went to Boston and became, according to himself, a first-class sinner. He had done almost everything that was bad, even to serving in "a house of ill fame," as he called it. He began reciting his evil deeds at once, went on and on to more and more grevious sins, began to sniffle and to wave a big handkerchief, and before long was really blubbering, shedding tears, and blowing his nose as his dreadful story developed. "But, praise the Lord," he said, "though my sins were black as coal and my guilt as red as blood, I am washed whiter than snow." That in an old-time Scottish Presbyterian pulpit! At that point, two elders, faultlessly dressed in long coats, came walking side by side up the aisle, just as they did when they went up for the collection plates, but this time they strode past the plates and the pulpit and turned one on each side of the evangelist. Then each took him by an arm and, without a word, marched him with continued dignity down the aisle and out the door.

Yet changes came so that before I left home for good I attended a service at which a one-time local boy, a highly respected minister, preached and afterwards asked people to come forward and declare themselves for Christ. Nevertheless, personally I mentally applauded the elders for what they did, and I still do. The old way, no matter what one thinks of it, commanded respect; this emotional nudism did not.

What happened while going to and from church was as interesting to us three children as what we did in church. One morning Duncan went off with the young horse, Dan, in the gig, while John ferried a boatload of neighbors across the lake to church. Alan went with Duncan and Colin and I went with Father and Mother in the buggy, which was drawn by Maud, our Morgan mare. We stood on the rear axle and hung on to the back of the seat. Father was grumbling about one of the wheel spokes rattling when a young man behind a smart and highly-decorated horse spanked past us in a cloud of dust— or rather, left us in a cloud of dust. Father said that he had better pay less attention to dressing up his horse and more to his farm. I am sure Mother was thinking of how little interest Neil himself took in his farm and cattle, but what she said was, "Oh, he is young and out looking for a wife, no doubt, and I do believe style is important to him." Father grunted. Before we got to the long, two-span bridge over the River Denys at Valley Mills there were several buggies before us and as many behind. By the time we joined the road from the River Denys Station we were in a long procession of vehicles. Now and then someone would drive past us, which made us fiercely jealous, and we urged father to let Maud do her stuff. He almost did once, and then thought better of it. When we got to MacAuley's store and home at Malagawatch, Mrs. MacAuley senior was getting into her grand carriage with the side lights and wide fenders and enclosed top. We were now on the south side of the lake, or our part of the Great Lakes, and the water between us and home was speckled with boats under sail. The most exciting way to go to church was by boat—it was trim and obviously faster. Boats were coming from the mouth of the River Denys, from Seal Cove, around Stoney Point from Orangedale, and from Gillis Cove. I wished I was in the bow of John's boat, my favorite place listening to the gurgling of water and watching the sails.

It was very improper to race boats on the Sabbath, but everyone did his best to be at the church landing first. Uncle Colin MacRae hove into view as we reached the church. He came from the opposite direction in a beautiful boat made by the same hands that made John's; its owner claimed it was the fastest on the lake. John had beaten him in a race once, and he took pleasure in reminding him of it.

This was the Sabbath of the "sacrament" season. Once a year in mid-June services began on Thursday, "the old man's day," when elders spoke on some topic agreed upon among themselves. Services were held daily through Monday. People from the whole general area worshipped together at these services— from River Denys Station as well as from Orangedale, Seal Cove, and Malagawatch, and from Little Narrows, Marble Mountain, Little Harbor, and Big Harbor. There were always several ministers, and generally more than one service going on at the same time.

This time there were two services outside and one in the church. The outdoor ones were much more fun. The following Sunday all the people would attend similar services in one of the other communities, and so on until all settlements in the enormous parish were served. This was Sunday, communion day, and the best-attended services, were, of course, on Sunday. Everyone was present, saints and sinners and all kinds between. It was the great social occasion of the year. Some people never did sit down, but wandered on the outskirts among the horses and buggies. The day was warm and sunny, and many parasols were raised. We had often heard of young swains throwing conversational candy at the girls, candies that bore such endearments as "I love you," "Be my girl," "Hello darling," "You're the girl for me," and "Be my beau." We had hoped that candy would be flying, and our hopes were fully realized. Candy bounced off parasols, missed their mark, and more often than otherwise were sternly ignored. Colin and I crawled on our hands and knees between the rows of people, and picked up many of the candies. We never had run into such a bonanza. Later, at home, it was vigorously impressed upon us that that was unseemly behavior. If one did something really wrong in my home, he was likely to do it just once. Anyhow, we hadn't realized that we were embarrassing our parents.

On such days many people called at our home for lunch, and the yard would be full of buggies and horses. We took as much pleasure in buggies and horses as kids today take in a yard full of cars, or in airplanes. The other day I watched a group of kindergarten children sitting by themselves on a lawn doing something when a huge bomber went over making a noise like the day of judgment, and the kids never looked up.

We busied ourselves during these days bringing hay from the barn for those who had not brought their own. Mother cooked as fast as she could, and then she and the girls served one table after another. The dining table seated about ten people, and I can recall five tables being served, not counting us young ones who ate leftovers in the kitchen. Mother often bemoaned the depletion of her stores after such an occasion.

Soon after this "Sacrament" Sunday, John, who was ferrying a woman across the lake, saw the monster that people had been excited about. It was rumored that it had been seen again in the lake, and it had been given all sorts of names, such as sea serpent, whale, and monster. And now John realized that it was more than a rumor. John was the least excitable member of the family, and we all believed him. He said the thing had surfaced right behind the boat. It had a flat head and something like a bristly mustache across its mouth. The head, he said, gave off a puff of misty breath that one could see and hear at some distance. Then the head went under, and right behind it there came up a big silver-colored barrel-like thing, and when it disappeared there came another and another. Then it would disappear altogether for a while before the head came up again. The following Sunday we started for church a bit early in the hope we might see the monster; we sailed all around Lewis Island and didn't see a thing. On another Sunday, however, most of the crowd that gathered along the Orangedale shores saw it, so probably not many people got to church at all that day. Hundreds of people from Whycocomagh, Alba, Little Narrows, and other places gathered for a look, and many were not disappointed. Most were afraid to go out in a boat to have a closer look, but John and a couple of neighboring young men went out and John took his gun. He said that more people would believe him if he shot the thing. They got near to it all right, and John shot bullets into it several times. When hit, it thrashed about and made a great whirlpool in the water and then disappeared, but after a while it would come up again and go on showing its head and its loops as though nothing had happened. Some people thought it was the Devil come as a judgment upon folks who went boat racing on the way to church.

The sea serpent advocates said they saw its tapered tail when it thrashed about. The idea of a whale was abandoned, since no one had ever heard of a whale shaped like this thing. One man from Newfoundland called it a Herring Hawk, and

50

said he had seen creatures like it along the Newfoundland coast. But no one ever really found out what it was, for it suddenly disappeared and was never seen again. A year later someone living near Marble Mountain reported that its skeleton had been found where it had gotten itself trapped in a shallow cove. A whale had been found trapped there once, and I remember seeing evidence of that whale; a Marble Mountain man used its jawbones as an arch over his front gate. The monster remained a mystery, however, and people thought the memory of the trapped whale suggested the story.

Colin and I misbehaved one night at the Orangedale Church. We weren't very old, and so maybe God forgave us even if the people did not. We had gone with Father and Mother and gotten separated from them at the church door, and so it happened that we sat by ourselves among people we did not know. The Rev. Mr. Rose was preaching, and he was in good form. We had often heard Colin Martin mimicking Mr. Rose's preaching, and we were delighted to find that his mimicking was just about perfect; the minister banged the pulpit just the way Colin Martin said. We could see a couple of flies buzzing about the minister's face; they must have been very distressing to him. He sensed that people had noticed, and his preaching got even more vigorous. He banged the right side of the pulpit and then the left, and waved his arms so that it looked as though he was shooing off the flies. Then he put both his clenched fists together and gave the Bible a fearful blow. Colin whispered, not too quietly, I am afraid, "He got one!" I snickered much too loudly. There was a terrible silence for a moment when everyone, including the minister, stared at us, and among all the eyes were those of Father and Mother. Another lesson was impressed upon our minds.

Mr. Rose came to call at our house soon afterwards. He had probably forgotten all about the snickering in church, but we feared that he had come to discuss our behavior and that we'd be in trouble again. He asked us about how we were getting on with the Shorter Catechism, as he always did, and no more. Then everybody sat in a circle, and Mother brought out the family Bible and set it before the minister. Mr. Rose read about the Prodigal Son, and afterwards we all got down on our knees with our elbows on the chairs while Mr. Rose prayed. When a minister prayed he wouldn't dare cheat his people with a short one, and so the prayer was long. I was curious and peeked through my fingers. Colin and Alan were peeking too, and Alan was getting red in the face as though he was about to giggle, but then Mother's eyes opened, and ours closed until the Amen.

When I was at home my feelings about the Sabbath were rather ambivalent, and I am sure Colin and Alan felt the same way. Most of the interesting things that happened happened on that day. The Sabbath gave us some backing in our natural desire to avoid work. We would have liked to have the Sabbath observance rule applied strictly to such tasks as cleaning stables, but cleaning stables fell into the category of "works of necessity and mercy." Colin said once that perhaps *we* should be shown some mercy. In any case, the Sabbath did not relieve us of much work, and it required a double load of chores on Saturdays. We had to haul in all the water that would be needed on Sunday—tubs and tubs of it, and it had to be pulled by the pailful from a forty-foot well and carried a hundred yards. We also had to saw and split enough firewood for the weekend, as well as bring it into the house and pile it neatly against the wall back of the stove. That stove had to be stoked constantly in winter, for it was the only source of heat in the house, except on occasion when the little heater in the dining room was lighted, and that happened only on very special occasions.

At night we undressed our feet in the kitchen and ran for the bed. The front hall was usually icy, with glittering frost on the walls by the stairs. We'd drop our pants on the way and dive into bed. Any prayers we might say were said under the blankets.

On Saturdays floors had to be scrubbed on hands and knees, and if the girls were busy at something else we'd have to lend a hand. In the barn hay and other feed had to be taken from mows and bins and set out so as to require the least possible labor in feeding the animals.

We did some playing on Sundays, but only because we could not be restrained all the time. If God made children and the Sabbath too, he was a bit inconsistent. We could get away with games played far enough from the house, and if they were the kind that could be played silently. On one Sunday morning I obediently sat on the woodpile behind the stove and counted my bare toes, wondering why they came in different lengths. Then I fished my old harmonica from a pocket and moved it silently back and forth across my mouth. Accidentally it gave a loud toot, and I was severely admonished. Later there was another accidental toot, whereupon the harmonica was put away for the day and I had to go and wash my feet, although they looked perfectly clean to me.

People played cards a lot in the evenings, and we children had the use of the old, dog-eared packs. We played with those on Sundays, if we wanted to bring the house down on us. The great disadvantage of the good day, was that so little that we wanted to do could be done.

Some early Sunday mornings when the weather was too bad for church, or something of the sort, Father read aloud from the Gaelic Bible. When he undertook to read he would lie down on the couch—a bench with a slightly upholstered denim covering. He used a special religious voice and tone which we thought he should have reserved for private devotions somewhere. Usually the reading terminated when he discovered that no one was paying any attention. He always seemed to choose a time when the rest of us had things to do that had to be done at once.

We went not only to church services, but also to the Orangedale Sunday School. We greatly enjoyed the dramatic stories, such as David and Goliath, Daniel in the lion's den, and Jonah and the whale, but the preachments were pretty meaningless. We were given leaflets so that we could prepare for our lessons, and each contained a scripture passage and a "golden text" which we were to memorize. Then there were questions about the passage and also the answers, which suggests that the appeal was exclusively to the memory.

The acceptability of Sunday School depended entirely on the teacher. I profoundly disliked the whole thing when Elder MacKinnon was our teacher, and that was because of what happened one day at his home, which was also the post office. I had been given letters to mail before school time. I walked right into MacKinnon's—at my home no one knocked as a rule, and if anyone did, he was almost certain to be a stranger or someone trying to be funny. It was quite different at MacKinnon's. As soon as I stepped inside I realized that I had made a great mistake. The family were all on their knees saying their morning prayers. I froze where I stood until they finished. Then the elder attacked me verbally for disturbing people at worship, elaborating on the discourtesy and thoughtlessness of my act. I could not see how pounding on the door could have been less disturbing. He was so angry that his face blanched and his hands shook, and I always afterward saw him wearing that face when I thought of him.

Stony John (John MacLean from Stony Point) was quite different. He couldn't have been more different. He was kind, he gripped us with his teaching, and he was always interested in us individually and knew all about us. He kept in touch with us until the day of his death. I loved Stony John, and I memorized reams of Bible verses for him. I once recited the entire Shorter Catechism and two hundred Bible verses to him, and for him, at one sitting. His pride knew no bounds, and that made me very happy. He was especially interested in Duncan Dan and me because of our interest in the ministry.

Duncan and I never wearied of talking about this ambition of ours. Going to school or coming home from school, on fishing trips, or on gum-picking walks in the woods, it was more often than not the topic of our conversation. Once we held a religious service of our own in Duncan's father's barn. The affair was more his than mine, although I agreed heartily with his plan. Duncan was more compulsively given to the idea of the ministry than I. I seemed to be destined for it by mundane circumstances, while Duncan was called. So he generally took the initiative. One day he posted a notice on the barn door inviting all kids to a church service on the following Sunday. Our parents were to be at one of those "Communion get-togethers" which we called the sacrament season, at River Denys, and the children were to be alone at home. The notice promised singing and a sermon. Duncan had brothers and sisters enough to make a fair congregation, and with Colin and Alan and me we'd make quite a crowd. Duncan's plan was that he should preach first, and I should preach at a similar service later.

It wasn't too easy to decide where in the barn to stage the show. There was the "barn floor," a big room into which horses pulled great loads of hay and oats. On each side there was a mow, one of which began about seven feet up while the other began at the ground. Above, where the roof began, foot-square crown-beams ran across from one side of the barn to the other. Our final decision was to seat the congregation on the edge of the wall above the deeper mow where they could let their feet hang down, and on the opposite side, up on the "crown-beam," the "minister" could take his stand, since this beam was the only thing that could suggest a high pulpit. The youngsters gathered in giggling anticipation of some fun, and then Duncan climbed on to the crown beam and announced a hymn. "Nearer My God to Thee" proved to be a bit difficult for us and so we tried "Jesus Loves Me," which we all knew, and it went remarkably well. I think all but Duncan and I expected something like Colin Martin's mimicking of Mr. Rose. But there was a prayer, and so everyone knew this was no play, and Duncan's eloquence surprised us all. When the prayer was done, he read from the Bible. He thought he would let the spirit guide him in the selection of a passage, and so he just let the book fall open where it would. Then he read something unintelligible about Jeroboam and placed the Bible between his feet on the beam. His preaching astonished us. He talked freely about the ninety and nine sheep, and we thought he did better than the "old men" on sacrament week. When he finished he raised his arm high in the air to pronounce the benediction, and the shift in his center of gravity unbalanced him so that he fell backwards into the mow behind him. The haying had just begun, and there was only a minimum of hay covering the loose poles. He completely disappeared into the hay. There was a clatter of loose poles followed by a great commotion in the hog pen down below; he

55

must have fallen all of twenty feet. We were stunned. Duncan might be hurt, and we had visions of death and tragedy. This was the Sabbath, on which pranks of any sort were forbidden.

In the meantime, Duncan found himself looking into the gaping mouth of an excited hog. He almost panicked, and then it occurred to him that he had done something no one had ever done before. He felt himself for broken bones and bruises, and when we got to him he was climbing out of the pen, grinning from ear to ear. A jubilant shout burst from all of us, and we raced back and climbed to the crown beam above the deeper mow in which there was much more hay. We had again discovered the unparalleled joy of jumping into the fresh-smelling hay, as farm kids have done ever since man began to store his fodder. God, parents, and church were forgotten, and so was preaching and the Sabbath. This climax to our first service was the reason why I never preached my sermon; fun had taken over. The fun, however, in no way deterred Duncan and me from the pursuit of our ambition.

OLDER THAN THE FAITH

I once listened to a conversation between two "liberal" clergymen, a Gaelic-speaking Scot and an Irishman who nostalgically talked about "the Little People," each assuring the other that he believed in them. They were lying to each other, of course, and each of them knew it. I think that what they were saying was that the Little People were necessary to them to keep them in touch with whatever is beyond the surface of reality. A letter from a friend who has a special interest in the Celt concludes with these words, in which he refers to a Celtic friend: " . . . who will have given the world another irreplaceable manifestation of the Celtic awareness of reality, or, to put it another way, the part of reality that, as I believe, only the Celts know."

There is at least a smidgen of Irish blood in this man, and that may be all there is to his conviction, but there may be more. One thing is sure, the Celt never takes life superficially. He may glory in it or fight its limitations like a Dylan Thomas, but he never ignores it or repudiates it, and is not likely to lose a sense of contact with the source of life or the controller of destiny.

After reading Eric Linklater's *The Survival of Scotland,* how can one talk of being Celtic? The mixture of bloods was considerable, but the Celtic peoples, nevertheless, never lost their identity. Anyhow a person such as myself who can find only Macs in his family tree has a right to call himself a Celt if anyone has. What I was about to say was that maybe what differentiates us is not cultural but comes out of our nature.

Speaking of the "Little People," however, I don't recall any reference to them in my family except once when Mother was telling us a dream she had had. "The hill out there opened up," she said, "and the Little People danced in and out. They had beautiful yellow hair and fat legs." We quizzed her about the "Little People," but all she said was that she knew about them, and "why should the world be for just our sort of people alone?" which at the time made me wonder if the dream wasn't more than a dream. The fact that Mother's Little People were blond, and that the word ban can mean blond makes me wonder about a possible kinship to the ban shidh, or banshee as we commonly say it.

All people have had their beliefs and still do—in dreams and ghosts and signs and miracles—but I wonder if the Celt wasn't more aware than other peoples of what I may call the underworld of the soul? Anyhow, pre-Christian beliefs and experiences were very much a part of the Cape Bretoner's life. Any reference to the supernatural agencies and events are always fascinating to any children and were especially to us, for to us all such things were realities, not just beliefs and notions. Most of what we heard of this underlying reality had to do with evil and with the foretelling of death and tragedy. Evil was not identified with a lapse in behavior; it was a positive, living power.

Once we saw a light wandering at the upper end of Uncle Dan's pasture, and the family and some guests watched it with an air of mystery and awe that gave it a sense of not being of our world. Someone noticed that the light was moving erratically towards Neillie John's home. Neillie was Ian Ban's son who was dying of tuberculosis. My brother Duncan suggested that "It's probably Uncle Dan out looking for a damn cow."

Lights usually gave notice of a coming death. We often heard of lights moving on the scene of some coming disaster or wandering periodically through vacant houses with a troubled history.

There were other signs too. A neighbor told of having the sheets on his bed pulled and tugged this way and that in the middle of the night. He lighted a lamp and searched his bed and room and found nothing, but as soon as he went to bed again the tugging on the sheets recurred. That was the night on which Ian Ban himself suddenly died, and it was said that the misbehaving sheets were used to cover the body.

Old Donald Cameron once showed me a lonely farmhouse beside a pond on the hills above the West Bay Road and told me a story about it, and this is what he said:

"Once a young man in that home had a fight with his father, who had deprived him of his heritage in favor of his brother, and he left home and went to sea. Some time afterwards he was drowned at sea, and his ghost began to appear on that pond. You might ask why on the pond? Well, remember the boy was a sailor, and so every time there was a heavy morning fog, people would hear the creaking of rigging and the flutter of sails on the pond, and just for a second as the fog was lifting they would get a glimpse of a magnificent ship under full sail. That went on for years, and maybe it still does; if anyone is living there to see it."

Mother told us once of dreaming of a crock of pirate gold under a tree near the Big Harbor beach which she knew very well. She induced her brother Christopher to go with her to dig it up. He dug until the tree was about to fall but found no gold. I used to think Uncle Christopher bungled the job, and I planned to dig up the crock when I got big.

Donald Nicholson told us preposterous yarns when he called, many of which went beyond the borders of natural phenomena. In the winter months we never saw him because the long Barren Road was filled with snow, but on the first warm day of spring he would walk to Uncle Dan's for the mail; Uncle Dan had acquired a post office. He carried a cane and wore an old cutaway coat, olive green with age. It was the dress and the time of Donald's appearance that led father to call him "The Dung-Fly." Father didn't like Donald very much, but we liked him and never missed teasing him into telling us some whoppers.

Once we had a sick cow for which we had given up all hope, and then she suddenly recovered. On Donald's next visit he received the story without surprise; he knew of such things. There was the case of a cow named Liza de Veau that he had gotten to know about while on a job near Riviere Du Loup in Quebec. Liza had died of malnutrition, and in January her carcass had been dragged across the ice in the river to a little nearby island and left there for the crows. In late March, after the ice had melted, a boatman found her alive at the water's edge. Although she seemed very shaky and stood on the tips of her frostbitten hooves, she was nursing a young calf. At this point Father snorted, and Donald said with some asperity, "say what you like, it happened that way, and I saw her with my own eyes being taken from the island to the shore on a raft." Father just rubbed the top of his head, as he always did when under tremendous tension.

There was the story of the newly-freshened cow that his son Peter had seen with a rabbit sucking at one of its teats. Peter had struck the rabbit with a rock, and it ran away with one leg dangling as if broken. Donald had a special falsetto voice which he used for such tales and in which he dragged out some words to ridiculous lengths. "A few days later," he said, "I met a woman from the backlands who was carrying one arm in a sling; she said she had broken it. Ye-e-e-es, broken it, and she wouldn't tell how it happened, but I had my o-o-own idea about how it happened." Donald believed in witches and the evil eye, and knew how cows dried up from an envious look, why hens quit laying, and why butter refused to gather in the churn. If there wasn't witchery in his yarns there was at least something miraculous. But Donald was really the kindest of souls, who never indulged in malicious gossip and never expressed ill will towards anyone. I think his superstitions were supported by a great love of the dramatic. Anyhow there was no harm in him.

He often claimed to have sailed the seas and told us once of a fish he had caught. He and his crew-mates were loading their schooner when, close by, a man hooked a fish that he couldn't handle. The fish was dragging him into deep water when several members of the crew went to his rescue and after a terrific struggle brought both fisherman and fish to shore. Donald called the fish a "caran Creagan"—some sort of rock fish. It was so big that a man six feet tall stood between its jaws with room to spare.

Once we had a terrible drought, and everything dried out and withered. John's beautiful horse was alone in the pasture across the cove, and the brook that watered all the cattle pastured there went dry without our knowing it. Mother somehow discovered that the horse was ill and brought him home; he had been drinking nothing but sea water for a week. Although a veternarian was brought all the way from Sydney, the fine animal died. While the horse was on his last legs Nicholson called and rebuked us for being so gloomy. There was still hope, he said; horse doctors don't know everything. He called for a wooden vessel, and mother brought him a homemade dish in which she set milk to cool in the cellar so the cream would rise. Then he wanted two sixpenny pieces and a shilling. Coins were collected from those who had some, and Donald was willing to accept two dimes and a quarter as substitutes for the sixpence and shilling. He put the coins in the bottom of the dish and covered them with a shallow layer of water; then he went to the stable and circled the dying animal, sprinkling it with water and mumbling some incantation to himself. He circled the horse three times, sprinkling all the while, and then declared that it would get well. "If that horse gets well I'll be ready to believe anything," was John's comment, but there were some signs of hope in his face. I believe that when people face disaster after doing their best with all the resources at their disposal they will go back to superstition rather than do nothing. Unfortunately the beloved horse died the night Donald thought he had cured him. The mound in the pasture where he was buried was a place to stand in solitary confrontation with what mattered most of all, and often I did.

Donald was not the only one who knew about old-time cures. I once saw a sick cow that hadn't eaten for days almost instantly cured; I believe it was a psychological cure. Three or four men discussed the cow's condition, and they must have agreed on a diagnosis. The cow was tied to a fence, and a man held her tightly by the neck until another man took a fish on a bit of string and, opening one of the cow's eyes so that the lower lid was turned inside out, hooked the delicate inside membrane and pulled out enough tissue to make it possible to snip off a bit with a pair of scissors. After that bit of tissue had been cut off, the cow, with blood running down its face, immediately began to crop grass.

Father had a number of the usual pre-scientific beliefs, such as that the spring planting, especially of potatoes and turnips, should be done during the decline of the moon if one didn't want to have all the growth go to the tops or foliage.

Some ancient things lingered on as play. When Father mowed hay with his hand scythe he would amuse us with a Gaelic rhyme to which the whetstones gave an accompaniment

> Winga, wanga, earball muice,
> Bogus lanta, bogus lanta.
> Winga, wanga, earball muice,
> Bogus lanta, bogus lanta.

In English it would be something like this:
> Winga, wanga, and a pig's tail,
> The lanta bug, the lanta bug.

Was that the echo of some ancient harvest incantation?

Some of his notions I never heard from anyone else. Scolding us for pointing a toy pistol at one another, he said that it might bring a "Devil's loan" of a bullet. We wanted to have more information about this lend-lease contribution from the Devil, but Father wouldn't say any more about it. This notion of his was possibly due to his concern about guns generally. Father never had an equal in instructing children about guns. We were allowed to go hunting partridges at a very early age, but we were first given some rigid tests. We learned how to pick up a gun from a boat in such a way that the hammer would not be lifted so that it could fire the gun, how to take a gun through a fence, how to carry a gun, and then how to leave it absolutely alone until we went hunting again. We really asked for trouble if we ever pointed a gun, loaded or not, at another person. But that was the first time we ever knew that the rule applied to toy pistols and heard about a Devil's loan.

Bellybutton Peg was a tall angular woman with the visage of one of the furies. She made the rounds occasionally like Big Charlie and other tramps, but she was no tramp; she never begged or expected food or lodging. She maintained herself somehow, although I never heard of her being employed anywhere. She would always berate almost anyone whose name happened to be mentioned—all were fools and scoundrels. She was very generous with her knowledge of cures for all sorts of ailments, and when giving instructions as to what to do, she softened and showed concern for the sufferers. She was a talker, and it was very hard for anyone else to say a word once she got started. She showed the whites of her eyes when she talked. One evening she arrived when we were all outdoors after supper. Colin had always been bothered with asthma, and on that occasion she heard him wheeze. Her eyes lighted up like torches, and she wanted to know what was being done for the boy. Mother told her that the doctor had given him some emulsified cod liver oil, and she snorted in disgust. "The boy can be cured," she said; "now I'll tell you what to do. Take him back into the woods far enough so that you can find a tree that he will never see again. Then stand him up against that tree, and with an auger bore a hole just above the top of his head into the heart of the tree. Then cut that cowlick off the top of his head and pack it into the hole. Plug up the hole with a good piece of wood, cut it off as you would a limb, and take the boy home. When he has grown past the hole the wheeze will be gone."

When she left there was a lot of laughter about Peggy's cure, but Colin and Alan and I met for a conference in the horse stable. We were all concerned about the wheeze; the cure could do no harm even if it didn't work and, who knows, it might work. So we got a kitchen knife, an axe, an auger, and, telling mother that we were going to pick spruce gum, we started out. I had the long auger down a pant-leg, which made walking rather difficult, but we didn't meet anyone before we got on to the highway. We walked about a mile up the Barren Road and then went into the woods. We wanted to be sure the tree we selected would be one Colin would not see again, and so we went a bit too far into the bush. We finally found a tree, a gnarled, old one in a dark hollow that people would be likely to avoid. We stood Colin against it, and I set the auger over the top of his head and started to bore. I did the boring because I was the tallest of the three, but even I had to get a piece of old stump on which to stand. Colin yelled every little while because I was catching his hair in the auger. Then we got a piece of tree-limb and whittled out a plug. Alan undertook to cut off the Cowlick, and pulled Colin's hair so much that he declared he would just as soon have the wheeze. We had trouble getting the stiff hair to stay in the hole, but finally managed and drove in the plug. Colin himself cut off the wood that stuck out with one blow of the axe, so that it looked as though someone had chopped off a limb. We started for home with full confidence, and after ten minutes of rapid walking I, fortunately in the lead, called a halt. I told Colin to "face the other way quick." I could see our tree again; we had gone in a circle. We had heard of people going around in circles in the woods and we guessed we were lost. We set out again, trying harder to go in a straight line but we went in a circle just as before. After doing this a third time we got into a heated argument over which way to go. My suggestion finally prevailed because it was the only one that was different from what we had tried; I said we should try our best to make a circle in the opposite direction, and that in that way we might trick ourselves into going in the right direction. We did, too; we lost the tree for good and found ourselves in a piece of burnt land that we recognized although it was all of two miles from home, because we had planted potatoes in it once after a fire had destroyed the trees. It was almost a little island in a loop of the river which passed our home.

We were afraid that Colin would not grow any more or that he might grow too slowly, and so we were most generous with him at the table for a while, something which Mother remarked about but didn't understand. In about a year Colin was rid of the wheeze, and we remembered Bellybutton Peg with deep respect—that is, until we overheard Mother telling about the boy's improvement and saying that children sometimes grew out of such ailments.

Peculiar to the Highland people is the gift of "the second sight," and it comes to only a few of them. Those who have it can see death and disaster in advance. Murdoch Martin, a quiet, kindly man who was also deeply religious, was credited with having the second sight. There was a story of how once he stared sorrowfully at a boy, saying, "The poor laddie, the poor laddie!" just before the boy's untimely and unexpected death. One spring Murdoch worked with Father and Uncle Dan at reclaiming some old machinery from the sawmill, which had fallen into disuse. I was asked to run some errands for them and was terrified lest Murdoch should fix his eyes on me. The dark powers could not be ignored.

Colin Martin, the jolly young man who used to mimic the minister and whom we liked so much, suddenly learned that he possessed the power. "Begod" was walking the highway with him one night, and he suddenly pulled Begod off the road and removed his hat saying, "Whose funeral can that be? And who ever heard of a funeral at night?"

Begod was amazed. "What has come over you, Colin? If it's drunk that you are, you are mighty stingy with the liquor."

Colin was still staring at the road. "A coffin drawn by two horses, and twenty buggies! You didn't see anything?"

"No, and begod, there wasn't anything. Man, it is cursed with the second sight that you are."

Even the ungifted were at times confronted with the emissaries of another world. I have already told how the Devil appeared to a drunkard. It may be to the drunken Highlander's credit that he never has a vision of God or the angels—it is always the Second-in-command who appears to him, and he could appear in any shape or form. I myself as a young child claimed to have seen him in the form of a blazing fire in the guest bedroom. I was alone in the house, probably a little scared, and the evening sun slanting into the room suggested the form of the appearance. What probably fired my imagination was that the dog, Purdy, raced into the room barking furiously, and immediately came out with his tail between his legs. He was probably ashamed of himself for barking at nothing, but I supposed he had been cowed by something he had seen. More interesting than my imagined vision was the response my story evoked from the family. They listened very seriously, asked a few questions, and just glanced at each other. There was no suggestion of disbelief, and although I am pretty sure that they suspected the truth, one never knew when something beyond nature, as we knew it, might be making contact with us.

Father had a momentary feeling that he was facing His Satanic Majesty one very dark night. He was coming home from a party with some cronies right after a torrential rain, in darkness so dense that he could not see anything at all, and as he floundered through the mud and puddles there was something white in the shape of a man's white shirt-front right close to him. He stood and addressed the thing in his best English: "It's a very dark night, that it is." There was no response. Then he tried the Gaelic with the same result; he had probably had a couple of drinks and didn't take too kindly to the silence. "It is warning you that I am," he said, and drove his pile-driver fist at the thing, and all hell broke loose. Mud and water were sprayed all over him, and the sound of hooves enlightened him. It was Uncle Dan's white-faced mare.

I can tell tales of superstitious beliefs, but I cannot begin to do justice to this other worldliness in the mental climate in which I grew up. Although we were not harried by spirits as many people have been, we did live in two worlds, and this second world answered many questions that baffle us in more enlightened and sophisticated times.

OUR BELONGING PLACE

Home was a place. We left it and came back to it. We knew where to find it. It was where we were fed, where we slept and were comforted, where we were judged and corrected, spanked and treated most tenderly; where we fought, faced our frustrations, and at times knew want and dread. I don't think I would live my childhood over again if I were given the chance, but neither would I exchange it for the life of children I know now. I would take it on again were it not for the difficulty of getting an education. And in any case I deeply cherish the memory of that bit of earth where I began to have my being. It was my time and my place, my bit of earth, my people, my dogs and horses and cattle. It was mine more than any other place on earth ever could be.

There was the house, every cranny and corner of which is still as familiar to me as my own body. Opposite the house, at the other end of the farm yard, was the barn with its animals that were its own kind of people, and beyond that were the path to the shore and the railroad bridge. On the north side of the yard was the buggy house, and opposite it the path to the old mill, along which we took the cattle to water. There was the balm o'Gilead tree with its fluttering leaves and its sticky, pungent buds, and the little apple orchard with its pink-fleshed red Astrakhans. This was our belonging place, I remember every little detail of grasses and bordering fences, the wood pile, the grindstone and sawhorse. Every inch of the insides of the buildings, the two great barn floors and the mows between, the shapes of boards and hatches and beams, and even rat-holes and snaggy nails with which I associated experiences that remained in my memory forever as they were when my senses responded to them. All these things composed the arena of our family life.

When we went to school we often took too much time on the way home, unmindful of the chores to which we were supposed to hurry back. There was always something that had to be done. Whoever coined the saying, "all work and no play makes Jack a dull boy" overlooked a child's ability to find some fun in almost anything he has to do, even in distasteful tasks. Except in the summer, the stables had be be cleaned daily, and the cow stable rarely failed to impress us with its distastefulness, but even that chore at times suggested amusing pranks.

One late winter's afternoon Alan and I were slowly getting on with cleaning the stable when I remarked on the gentleness of a certain Jersey cow under which I was spreading some straw. I told Alan that I bet him I could crawl right under her. He took me up on it, of course, and so I got down on all fours and crawled under. I had not thought of the wild-eyed ox-like creature standing next to her on the far side. The moment that stag of a cow saw my head appearing from under the Jersey she kicked me right on top of the noggin. I was knocked out instantly. My first consciousness found me out in the snow with Alan standing over me in great concern. I was filthy with cow manure, bleeding from nose and ears, and one of my eyes was swollen shut. I must have been kicked more than once. Alan had dragged me by the feet the whole length of the trough and out the door into the snow. A ridge was growing on the top of my head, which still remains. They used to tell me later that the cow had done me a good turn by cracking my skull so that my brain could grow some more. That was in explanation of my subsequent superior work at school.

On another occasion I was nearly gored. I had been told to take our cow Dandy's calf away from her for weaning. I did so and got the little one comfortably stalled. Then I got him to drink some warm milk from a bucket by first letting him suck my fingers, then dipping his nose along with my fingers into the milk, and finally gently withdrawing my fingers. Later that evening I was taking an armful of wood into the house and had just gone up the steps to the porch at the moment when Colin was passing by with the cows which he had brought from the pasture. Dandy spied me and came for me like a demented thing. I just had time to drop the wood, slap down the door latch, and fall across the doorstep when Dandy went past me like a blur of fury; she went clean through the end of the porch. Someone said that I had had a demonstration of mother love, but I thought it was just a mean old cow.

Perhaps the most distasteful task was taking cows that were in heat to the bull. Sometimes we did not have a bull of our own, and we had to take the lovelorn animals to a neighbor's bull. The embarrassment of having to ask for this service was profound, but something funny nearly always happened which partly redeemed the chore. Once we went to the pasture to pick up a lovesick animal and found that a huge strange bull had anticipated our intention and had crashed through the highway fence. He had already served the cow in question, and then seemed determined to rape every cow in the pasture. The herd apparently thought this improper, for they ganged up on him and butted him back through the fence into the highway. We drove him away, but felt most grateful to him for making our chore unnecessary.

My sister Flora and I once went to bring the cows home for milking. They were across the river in the pasture that bordered the cove, and we had to drive them to the west end of the farm to find a bridge. This time our own bull was guarding the herd. He had never shown any signs of viciousness, but even a bull as tame as a tabby cat can suddenly become dangerous, and this one did. He came upon us in a scrub-filled area before we found the cows, and made no secret of his violent intentions. I picked up a stick and swatted

70

him over the head, but the stick broke in pieces and did no damage. We ran and the bull ran after us. Every time I found a stick I turned and gave battle, but every stick I picked up was old and rotten. So we fought and ran, fought and ran, and in a direction away from home. Finally we came to a fence bordering Donald Og's property. It was a new five-rail fence but we didn't have time to climb over it. When we reached the cove we found that the fence ran quite a way out into the water to keep the cattle from walking around it. Wading was our only hope, and so we plunged in up to our necks. When we gained the other side we relaxed and started home without our cows, but as we climbed the style over the railway fence the bull was on our heels again. He had somehow gotten through the rail fence, but we were safe enough, for the railway had two fences, which would give us time enough to get across the river on the log bridge we often used. Next day father put a ring in the bull's nose, and soon after he sold him to the butcher.

The only thing I liked to do with cows was to poke the hay to them through the hatches in the morning. They greatly relished it, and blew blasts of sweet-smelling breath at me. A cow's breath was something to wonder at.

We helped mother do the milking as soon as we were able, but she could milk two or three cows while we were milking one, and she supervised us rather severely as to cleanliness; milk tasting of the barn was an unspeakable disgrace.

In winter we took the cows for water to the creek once a day and the horses twice a day. We usually had to shovel a path through the snowdrifts on the brow of the creek's embankment. On sunny, warm days the animals were allowed to go free in the yard.

One spring we found a cow in the act of delivering a calf. Mother was away shopping, and no one else was around either. The calf came cornerways and stuck fast. We were in a panic. Something had to be done, and we could think of nothing but to pull the calf free. Covering our hands with gunnysacks for a better grip, we pulled and tugged, but to no avail, and we were about to give up when the cow gave a mighty heave just as we pulled, and the delivery was accomplished. The young one was a miserable-looking thing, but we worked it into the cow's stall and she began to clean it up. Then we gave her a bucket of warm water generously sprinkled with corn meal, as we had seen mother do on other occasions.

Then the afterbirth scared us. Had we turned the poor animal inside out? Luckily someone came home and assured us that everything was quite normal, and even congratulated us.

We loved the horses and never dreaded cleaning their stables; the stuff wasn't messy. Gordon was a gray draft gelding—a quiet, obedient, and gentle creature most of the time, though sometimes he bit us when we went up beside him in the stall while he was feeding. For some unknown reason Colin suffered most from his bites. We believed that Gordon was strong enough to out-pull any horse in the neighborhood. Maud, the Morgan mare, never displayed any sign of irritation or unwillingness while she was in harness, but when on occasion she got loose in the stable she would back up to Gordon and just about kick the hide off him, and would not stop until someone came to the rescue. Maybe that was because once her newly-born foal went and stood in the stall beside Gordon, and he was so flattered that he tried to keep everyone away from it. Gordon was rather defenseless. He couldn't kick, and so he would just bob his rear end up and down. Maud could kick anything from the floor to the ceiling with the greatest accuracy. John's Dan was attended to by one of the older boys when any of them were around; otherwise we groomed, fed, and watered him, but were not allowed to harness or drive him.

In summer we had the added chore of bringing a horse in from the pasture when one was needed. Gordon often objected to being taken in, and one morning Colin took a pan full of oats just to make sure. Gordon refused to come near him, but Colin put the pan on the ground and stepped back, and Gordon immediately came forward and began to eat. Colin then confidently stepped forward, but Gordon resented

72

being taken for a nitwit and flattened back his ears, bared his teeth, and reared straight up, waving his enormous hooves within inches of Colin's face. We had to herd him home that day as though he were a cow.

Maud always tried to dodge us, but she could always be caught with some oats and she would stand still if we got her into the corner of a fence. But horses are like people; they don't always behave consistently. She was in a very negative mood the day Colin had his John Peel ride. She turned away every time Colin was about to reach for her mane. He had brought neither halter nor bridle, let alone oats. He grew tired and a bit irritated at her dodging, and so he picked up a bit of a stump root, and, hiding it behind his back, approached her again. He knew by now just when she would turn away, and so instead of taking the last step he leaped at her, grabbed her mane and jumped on her back, helped by her sudden forward movement. Then he wacked her with the root, and immediately she went into high gear. He had nothing with which to steer her, and she galloped fiercely toward the highway. When she got to the fence bordering the road she went over it like a bird and then across the road and over the fence on the other side. These were five-rail fences, but she went over them without so much as touching them and then had a great run across a green meadow in the direction of Uncle Dan's place. At the far end of that field there was not only a fence but a big ditch beside it. Maud cleared them both and raced up to Uncle Dan's front door where Aunt Mary was standing. Here she stopped and blew a great blast of breath. Colin rapped her again with the root, and she whirled and went back over all the fences again, and still another on the way to the barn. She stopped at the barn door, and then snorted as if immensely pleased with herself. How could a kid riding bareback hang on? You ask me. All I can say is that Colin always had surprising reserves.

One season we took up cock-fighting, a sport of which we had never heard. We began by just taking sides in a cock-fight. That spring there was an unusually large group of young roosters, and they naturally fought as they grew up. Soon each of us identified ourselves with a particular rooster. The first one that I claimed was white, and he won most of his fights.

He was about to be declared champion when a cow lay down on him in the night and slept on him until morning. He was as flat as a dinner plate when we found him. I had to select another, and the one I selected turned out to be no good at all. Like some people, he was quick to start a fight but would run as soon as he met real opposition. According to the rules we had set up, we could not get rid of a bird while it lived and was able to fight at all. Colin had a big black cock that won all his fights and was soon strutting about, the master of the farmyard. Alan's was a speckled pepper-and-salt bird with fine spirit, who could handle any bird except Colin's black.

Then something happened that spelled doom for the black. Alan Mohr (Big Alan, Donald Og's carpenter son) came to call one evening carrying an enormous cock under his arm. It was a present to Alan Bec (Little Alan). As Alan Mohr presented it he said to Alan Bec, "Just try that one, and I'll be very much surprised if you don't have a champion."

The bird was twice the size of any of our birds and as beautiful as a peacock. He had two-and-a-half-inch spurs that were as sharp as needles. Our cocks, not having been bred for fighting, had practically no spurs at all—they just pecked.

When Alan let his prize bird loose, the bird made straight for Colin's black champion, and with one jab of his spurs left him half dead. He went through all our other cocks in less than a day, killing one and crippling most of the others. Then he strutted about, flapping his wings and crowing, but no bird took up his challenge. Then, bored with that, he ran back and forth in a disgruntled state, until he spied the ducks. These quiet birds fed in the creek by day, and came home in the early evening all in a row behind the drake. They had just reached the barnyard when the great cock noticed them. The drake was a docile, gentle thing, dressed in white, and never had to put up a fight. The big rooster made for him, leaped up, and clapped his deadly spurs together, but missed. He repeated the same tactics with the same result. The duck could duck, and made a very bad target. The cock thought this wouldn't do at all and closed in, throwing his spurs about but hitting nothing. Then the drake decided he had ducked long enough, grabbed his assailant by the wattles and hung on.

74

The cock looked embarrassed. Duckie then began to back away, dragging the cock after him. His web feet had good traction; the rooster dug his spurred feet into the ground and reared back, but nothing he would do could stop the duck's progress. The duck dragged him clean around the barn and was on his way around the second time when people began to notice the strange combat and gathered to watch. I think it must have been the loud laughter that made the duck nervous enough to let go. But the great game-cock was already through. He turned and ran. Duncan remarked, "The damn fool! He tackled something he knew nothing about." Father observed that that was the fate of all bullies; sooner or later they overreach themselves. The bird had been improperly matched, and it was a tragedy. Now, even the hens would peck at him, and with no rooster to put up a fight any more, the fun went out of cock-fighting.

Sheep are uninteresting creatures as a rule, but even they can provide their quota of excitement. We had a huge ram that must have weighed three hundred pounds. When young, he had been teased and pestered by some boys who had destroyed the sight of one of his eyes. After such experiences any human being was fair game for him, and he would attack on sight anyone who came into the same field with him.

It was a day of fun for us when he got into the driveway just as a heavily-burdened peddler was approaching the house. The peddler dropped his packs, leaped the fence, and watched the packs being butted to pieces. The big bundle which held clothes and towels and such, didn't respond to the ram's satisfaction, and so he turned his attention to the square box that we called the jewelry box. It split open at the first bunt, and the ram tossed it about with great satisfaction. Mother soothed the man with apologies and food as we children collected his goods. We didn't get them all, for we kept picking watch chains, cuff-links, thimbles and needles out of the dust of the driveway for weeks.

Someone told Duncan that when a ram came for him all he had to do was to lie down on his belly to make the animal lose all interest in him. With this bit of wisdom Duncan entered the field with the ram and found out that there was at least one ram who didn't care whether a man lay down or stood up. He was thumped on the rump by this enormous hunk of horned fury, ran as he probably never did before or since, and vaulted the fence just inches ahead of catastrophe. Thus the beast was worthy of the respect in which he was held by everyone who had made his acquaintance.

Soon after my eleventh birthday Donald Cameron from West Bay road came in search of a boy who would fetch and carry for him during the summer months. I was chosen, and so rode with Cameron in a rickety old buggy over the eighteen or twenty miles to West Bay Road. I didn't just fetch and carry for him; I worked like a man, and did even more than the men who worked with me. I generally packed the hay on the wagon while two husky men pitched it to me, and I soon learned the art of building the hay load out over the wheels, out behind, and forward to the middle of the horses' backs. When the hay was hauled into a barn or a stacking place (four upright posts with a pyramid roof that was raised or lowered as need dictated), I was transferred to the mow where I spread and stamped down the hay. That was the most arduous job in the whole haying business. When we got home in the evenings the men washed up, relaxed, and filled their pipes, and I brought the cows in from pasture and helped Mrs. Cameron with the milking. In the morning I was the first one up, and started the fire in the stove. Once I woke up and, seeing a light in the neighbor's window, supposed it was getting-up time. I had the fire blazing when Mrs. Cameron appeared in great amazement—it was eleven o'clock at night! In the mornings after attending to the fire and getting the kettle on, I went to the pasture again for the cows and helped with the milking. It was a hard summer.

I mention this break in the routine of my life to tell of my experience with the rams. Cameron brought home a beautiful pair of them from somewhere, probably to improve his stock. He had them tied together by the neck with a piece of chain, and asked me to hold them while he went to the barn for a tethering rope. While getting the rope, he knocked a box of scrap-iron from a beam with a great bang and clatter. That was all the rams needed. They started off, and I might as well have tried to hold the north wind as those animals. One of my fingers got caught in a link of the chain so that I didn't dare to let go—all my weight on that one finger would have torn it off. They dragged me a good half mile, right through a boggy place below an overflowing spring, and got me thoroughly soaked and muddied up. Reaching a fence by the woods they circled and galloped back, and on the way entered a corral into which the cows were gathered night and morning for milking. The corral was covered with bovine excreta, and I think I was dragged through every bit of it before they found the gate again. All the while they were dragging me they kept on stepping on my hips and thighs with their sharp hooves, and I was well on the way to the bog-hole once more before I was able to reach the chain with my other hand and release my trapped finger. I was bleeding badly when I got back to the house and Mrs. Cameron began apltying a remedy which hurt worse than the wounds. But I was given a day off and some personal attention, which I appreciated.

Cameron had an insane man working for him—the man was crazy as a coot in some ways, but a good worker and most tender and solicitous towards me. He took over the bandaging, saying, "I'm coming through the doctoring." He always said that he was coming through whatever he did. I'm coming through hoeing the potatoes," he would say, or "I'm coming through splitting wood." When eating, he would say, "I'm coming through the hash." He entered a door or gate as if he were driving a horse and cart through it; he would take a wide turn so as not to bump his imagined vehicle on a door jamb or gatepost. Once I saw him closing the two huge barn doors so that he could use the little door set in one of the bigger ones.

He was so concerned about me on that morning that Cameron came storming up to him in anger for leaving his job, and, taking him by the throat, slammed him several times against the wall. Cameron had once been a guard at the insane asylum in Mabou and was at times given charge of harmless men for the work he got out of them. Hughie kept muttering as he took up his work again, "The lad was bleeding. I was coming through with the doctoring."

I went to Cameron the following two summers—God knows why, unless it was because of the suggestion of maturity in going away to work. The wages were no inducement, for all I got that first summer was a pair of blue denim pants, and a pair of hobnailed shoes. I was given a straw sailor hat the second summer. It had a ribbon around the crown with the words "H M S Ophier" on it. I didn't believe that anyone on His Majesty's ship would tolerate the thing for a minute. At the end of my third summer Mrs. Cameron gave me thirty-five cents.

In the early spring some lambs would come too early, and at times a lamb would be without a mother; these lambs would be brought into the house and fed. Mother would take one in her lap, fill her own mouth with milk, and squirt it into the lamb's mouth. In recalling this I am reminded of a poem by Tibullus in which a shepherd feeds a lamb in exactly the same way. At times one of the children would take on all the responsibility for a lamb, but the trouble with that arrangement was that the little lamb would follow whoever fed it like a puppy, bleating for more food. Flora once took care of one, and it was half grown before she could shake it off for as much as a minute. She would get furious at the thing, for people teased her about it. Even after it was put out to pasture with the flock it would worm its way through the fences to follow her again.

The worst about the sheep was the shearing, and attending to the male lambs in the late spring. Father spayed the little rams with a jack-knife and nothing but chewing-tobacco spittle for an antiseptic, yet not one ever got an infection. Mother did the shearing, and we all helped her wash the fleeces in the creek. This was an unhappy, smelly job but an essential one; socks and mittens and blankets were made at home.

There were some experiences not so delightful as most of those I have described. No language can adequately describe the feelings with which I responded to the family butchering. There was no escape from watching the killing, for anyone who tried to dodge the sight would be branded a sissy. So I looked on while pigs were stabbed with a long knife and allowed to walk about while bleeding to death; I watched while sheep were held down and their heads severed with a knife without benefit of any stunning, shooting, or other anasthesia. The cows and steers were more mercifully handled, being first struck over the head with a sledge hammer before being bled. There were some advantages to all that; I was saved from the false delicacy so common now, made possible for us by the great meat-packing industries who do the killing for us. There was also something festive about it. Soon after the bad day we'd have sausages, in which we delighted. They were made with cows' intestines, which were most rigorously cleaned, being turned inside out several times and soaked. Later they were filled with delicious stuff, and the odor of those sausages being fried made a red-letter day of almost any day.

Even funny things happened. Male calves were butchered after they acquired some flesh, and there came the time when the kids did the job if it was to be done. I remember Alan volunteering to butcher a calf for its hide; he was in desperate need of money. He went to the stable with his tools, but after a little while the calf came racing out the door and headed for the hills, with Alan after him with an upraised hammer. I eventually did the job myself and let Alan have the hide. I could do anything that had to be done, even if it did bring its horrors.

I finally blamed God for the whole business. The fang and claw were adequate evidence of what he intended, and I took an oath that I would never eat flesh that I could not prepare myself.

Swimming was one of the joys of summertime. There was some nice white sand in relatively shallow water at Uncle Hector's Point, and that is where we usually stripped and went in, garbed in our God-given bathing suits. It was a lovely place to swim except that in the bottom grew a lot of oysters, and we often gashed our feet on their razor-sharp shells. One of the times was memorable because after the three of us came out of the water we found that our clothes had been taken. We suspected Duncan, and we were right. We began an advance in the direction of home that might have done credit to guerrilla warriors, slipping from bush to bush in great fear of being seen. We felt a shyness about sex that made this a fearful trip. When we got to the railroad we could see the yard of our home, and to our horror a stylish horse and buggy told us that there was a guest. I was so mortified that I howled and Colin looked as if he would join me, when Duncan appeared with our clothes. He had been hiding under the end of the bridge. "Next time," he said, "you should take your clothes off nearer home." When we got to the house we found that the guest was the minister. After that experience I didn't mind hiding my face against a chair-bottom while Mr. Rose prayed.

In no other spot on earth would we ever again live so intensely as we did in that farmyard. The joys of life there transcended all joys, the griefs and frustrations were deeper than anywhere else on earth. No hopes or dreams could be so extravagantly sweet as in that place, no love so reassuring, no life so complete.

ONCE THERE WERE SEASONS

As the author of Ecclesiastes says, "For everything there is a season, and a time for every purpose under the Heavens." So it was until the demons of speed and refrigeration began to destroy time. With us there was a time for strawberries and cream, a time for eating oysters fresh from the water, a time for new potatoes and apple picking, a time for butchering and sausages, a time for almost every kind of fresh fish or meat, a time to go barefooted and a time for feasting and a time for tightening belts, a time for horse-racing and for skating, a time for swimming and for being tubbed— yes, a time for every purpose under the sun.

I think it was in the fall of 1902 that winter weather anticipated the season a bit. The hay and oats filled the mows and the potato crop was in the cellar, but we had not yet begun to thresh the oats; the sheep had not been brought in from the pasture beyond the river nor had the butchering been done. The fish-nets were still out; we "ran" them every morning, and we kids helped John on weekends to rake up and sort oysters which he would sell. Fall activities would be attended to in a leisurely way when it began to snow. Father was somewhere near the mouth of the River Denys running the codfish nets when the first heavy flakes settled around him. The flakes thickened and so increased in force that he decided to pull up the nets for the season. Before he had them stowed away there was a thick layer of snow in the water that didn't seem to melt. The snow dragged on the boat when he began to row, and before he got half-way home it was extremely hard to move and he and the boat looked like a piece of snow sculpture. Before he got into the cove he was making almost no progress at all. When he managed to reach a net pole that stuck out of the water he pulled it free. It was all of twenty feet long and as heavy as lead, but he thought it might be more effective than the oars. Raising this enormous cudgel, he would bring it down on the layer of snow with a tremendous smack and a backward thrust toward the stern. The boat responded very slowly, but it did respond. It took him two hours to do the last mile. When he got to shore we could not see him until he was almost upon us. Alan Mohr had come to tell us that Father was on the way, for he could be seen from Alan's place for almost the whole distance he had to travel. When he stepped out of the boat he staggered; Mother anxiously put out her hand to steady him, but he growled her away. Father had a forty-four inch chest, a seventeen-inch neck, and legs like pilings; if it hadn't been for these assets he never would have made it. At the house Mother brought out a bottle of Scotch whiskey, which was rarely used except for guests and in cases of illness, and made a huge pitcher of hot toddy, and he drank it all and went to bed. He was asleep instantly.

Rod MacDonald, a cousin of Mother's from Marble Mountain, drove in at dusk. Both man and horse were tuckered out from floundering in the snow. We were thinking of bed sometime later when a wail from Mother, who was in the basement, startled us all. We were afraid she had hurt herself, but almost at once she pulled herself up through the hatch in the floor which was our access to the basement in winter. "The sheep!" she moaned, and then we all moaned. We had all forgotten the sheep. They were in the pasture across the river and would be buried in snow even if they could be located, or they would have taken to the scrub for protection and might never be found in time. Mother was for getting them right away in the dark and storm, and could not be dissuaded until MacDonald opened the door and told her to take another look at the weather, which was getting worse by the minute. After that, she gave up the sheep for lost.

In the morning the snow was over everything. The roads were blocked to the tops of the fence rails, and the railway was in even worse condition; the cuttings at each end of the bridge, one of which was at least thirty feet deep, were completely filled with snow. Not a train moved for almost a week. Colin Martin and Neillie Malcolm (whom we called Begod), joined us during the night, saying they wanted to see the storm through with us. Ordinarily they would have found a place to sleep and would not have disturbed anyone, but on that night they were wet and exhausted, and Mother had to get up to get them hot food and some dry clothing.

In the morning Mother had to help us clear a narrow path to the stables where she milked, and we helped as well as we could. As she worked, she worried out loud: "The sheep, the poor sheep! The flour is almost gone and there is no meat at all, the salt cod your Uncle Colin was to send hasn't come yet, the few fresh cod we have won't last more than the day with so many people to feed, and the little butter I put by will go too." We told her that she was being too pessimistic and I am sure she felt she was exaggerating, but all she said turned out to be true. This was no early snow-flurry that would melt in a day or so. A little snow was still falling and the temperature had taken a dive. As Mother said, it was cruelly beautiful.

Mother roused out the men to go and see about the sheep. They organized a party and, after eating, started out. The job took them all morning, for they had to carry each sheep a good half mile and across the railway bridge. They brought them all in, though one was dead and frozen stiff; the dead one had gotten frozen to the limbs of a fir tree under which it had sought shelter. The others were found all huddled together and almost completely buried. Rod MacDonald had the dead one properly skinned and cleaned, and he did it all on the kitchen table. "Who would be stupid enough to let meat like this go to waste?" he said, and Mother approved. Colin Martin and "Begod" had given noble service in rescuing the other sheep, for which Mother was grateful. But guests along with the family! Food was going to be scarce.

That night Mother was up late baking her last batch of bread. The flour barrel was empty and there was no telling when it could be refilled. What would she do when the bread was gone? But there were always those hard-time rations that few people were ever caught without: brined herrings and boiled potatoes. When she went to bed she came to look at us —Colin and Alan and me—in the big old, red-painted pine bed. I pretended to be asleep as usual; she carefully tucked in the blankets and the light receded.

Sometime during the morning Alan Mohr came again, this time on snowshoes—the only pair in the community. People loved to visit when something unusual occurred. Johnnie Hector came too, after practically swimming his way through the snow; he had a bottle and wanted to borrow some kerosene, and his mother, Aunt Jessie, would also like a couple of teaspoons of soda for a bannach, and a cup of sugar. He said the storm had found them without supplies.

We younger folks were happy with the whole show. The snow was marvelous, and most of the time we were soaking wet from floundering in it. There were lots of people and a lot of talk, and stories of other storms and disasters, which we loved. Cold and exertion made everyone hungry, and food disappeared as fast as Mother prepared it. In a couple of days the bread was gone, and mother's worry increased, but then she thought of something. She went to the barn, and on her return began mixing things. At the expected breadless supper she brought in hot, flat brown cakes which everyone pronounced delicious. Where did she get anything to make them with? She proudly announced that she had used bran from the bin in the barn. And that was how we discovered that bran was good for people too.

Then men working with huge, scoop-like shovels appeared on the highway; they were clearing a way for horses and sleds. By the time horses could flounder their way through,

84

Mother's larder, including the small supply of wild fruit she had preserved, was bare. But traffic began to move, the winds and tides began clearing the icy snow from the cove, and life began to be fairly normal again.

It was usually well into December before the time for eel-spearing came. By then there would be an inch or two of ice on the cove, and all the men of the neighborhood would gather the yearly crop of hibernating eels. We kids could not use spears, but were busy and excited observers. The men used long, light poles attached to iron spears, and poked in the muddy bottom for the eels, which had dug in for the winter. One could easily tell when one struck an eel. When the spear hit one, the men would run in a direction away from the hole until the eel and spear came up. The fish was easily scraped off, and then the poking would be resumed. Old Donald Og, his sons Olan and Laughie, his brother Murdoch, my brother John, and others were there, and they soon had the selected area honeycombed with holes a yard wide. Around each hole were many eels that squirmed awhile and then froze. The climax of the day was when Laughie Donald felt his spear catch on to something big, ran backwards in his desire to see his prize eel appear, and suddenly stepped into an abandoned hole. He would have "shut the door," as the lumberjacks in Maine used to say, if it hadn't been for the spear pole. He was speedily dragged out along with his champion eel, which was enormous, and everyone enjoyed his mishap. He kept saying, "O Mother, Mother," as he spiked eels onto a wire by inserting it through their ears, and then started for home, dragging his catch behind, his frozen pants crackling as he went.

Something that delighted me and no one else was the discovery that the ice was so clear in places that I could see fish swimming about below. The ice was so thin and elastic that it bent under the men and creaked as they walked about. They said it was not as brittle as the ice on fresh water.

For many days people feasted on eels as sweet as any that ever swam. Our folks didn't like them when cured in any way they knew about, so they had to eat them within the time they could be kept in a snow bank. Winter spearing was soon given up because of the thickness of the ice; by the middle of January, as a rule, it would be eighteen inches to two feet or more thick. Then we could fish for smelts and speckled trout, which could be pulled through small holes.

I was always fishing. Mother persuaded me once to wear her red woolen bonnet, a thing that covered head and ears and neck, and part of the shoulders. She said the fish liked red and that the hood would be reflected in the water, and I never suspected that she was concerned about the cold. I was very lucky that first time, and ever afterwards I firmly believed that that hood attracted fish to my hole in the ice. I was just the most persistent. Anyhow, that red bonnet could be seen on the cove almost any time there wasn't any school. My faith in the red hood was supported by the fact that everyone put a bit of red wool on the hooks, beneath their bait. The wool was a very good idea, for one could catch smelts if they nibbled enough to get their teeth caught in the wool, and one merely had to ease them onto the ice before they could let go. Bill Miller once said that the red wool didn't help any, and I almost hated him for it.

Some people will question the idea of catching speckled native trout in salt water, yet trout do inhabit and feed in every cove I knew for miles around my home. We usually caught the bigger ones in nets after the ice had gone in the spring. There is no doubt about their being trout.

The great moment in my fishing career came one sunny day right after lunch. Time and weather seemed to be against me. Father said, "You'll not catch any fish in weather like this," and Mother said, "Noon time is a bad hour for fishing. Why can't you wait until between three and four?" I had a certain feeling, however, that to me was more trustworthy than any weather, and my answer was to slam the door behind me. I selected a new place opposite Uncle Hector's home, and close to the Monroe shore, where a tiny brook entered the lake. Cutting the hole was almost more of a job than I could manage. The ice was well over eighteen inches thick, and when I finally chopped through it the hole was no more than four inches in diameter at the bottom, although it was almost two feet across at the top. I lay down on my belly on the ice,

86

and with my nose almost in the water, watched the hook and bait as I bobbed them up and down with what I believed to be an irresistable wiggle. Between the ice and the bottom there was no more than fifteen inches of water, so that I could clearly see any fish that crossed the hole. Little "pin-fish" (sticklebacks) pecked at the bait, and once in a while they would get their teeth tangled in the wool and I'd have to take precious time to get them off. Nothing else appeared for a long time, and then the pin fish scattered and an agitated smelt dived at the bait. I knew such agitation meant a big fish somewhere near, and so I tried to dodge the smelt, but it finally hooked itself and, mumbling profanity, I would not dare to use at home, I pulled it up and unhooked it. As soon as I let the bait down again more excited smelts appeared, then suddenly they too fled, and the trout of all my dreams swam slowly past my hook. I wiggled the bait frantically, and after a while the big fish came again, and as it passed my hook it opened its mouth and sucked in the bait. I pulled fiercely on the heavy thing, and then the line broke right at the hook. A wave of despair hit me, and then I noticed that the trout had come up through the small end of the hole and was floundering in the upper and larger part. I drove my arms into the water up to the shoulders in an effort to catch it, but it evaded me. I got my hands down to the small entrance and swirled the water around, not knowing what else to do, and then the big fish leaped right onto the ice, slapping its tail against my face. It was enormous and I was in ecstasy. I grabbed it by the gills and, leaving axe and line right where they were, ran for home.

Everyone exclaimed with proper expressions of surprise and admiration. Father tried to weigh the fish on his huge steelyards, a scale that was used for weighing beef and grain; he estimated its weight as somewhere over five pounds. I crammed a bit of lunch into my mouth and, finding an extra hook, started out again. I fished the rest of the afternoon and caught two other large fish between one and two pounds in weight, and a number of others, but saw nothing that could compare with the first one. It was getting dark when I reached home. There was a strange horse and cutter in the yard, and dinner was over. Then I began to be aware of a situation that in a child's mind was lamentable, calamitous and tragic. The table was littered with leavings and conspicuously among them were the bones of my big fish; they had eaten all of it. Mother apologized and almost shed tears. She cooked and served me one of the other big fish, but it tasted like sawdust. I understood Mother's situation very well, but the tightness in my insides did not abate until everyone else was asleep and exhaustion overcame me.

A child revels in snow as a husky dog does, and so it was natural that winter should bring us unparalleled happiness. The hill on which our parents had built their log cabin was not exactly a thrilling place to slide, but it was good nevertheless. We had a home-made sled about four feet long with polished steel shoeing. John had had Uncle Hector make it for us. It would make the little sleds children generally use now look like toys, and it had weight enough to make it really travel. Close to the barn the river embankment was about forty feet above the stream and plunged down very steeply. The slope was too steep for the sled, and the snow usually formed cliffs that hung over beautifully. Here we slid on the seats of our pants, although it was forbidden. We always got soggily wet and wore the seats out of our pants, which soon developed patches and eventually patches on top of patches. We got dirty too, although I cannot explain how that could have happened in the beautiful white snow. But I do remember the black color of our sliding places. We'd begin by leaping at a fresh cliff and would go right through it, letting an avalanche of snow bury us below. Repeated jumps made slides which grew more and more slippery; these slides would get discolored worse than the slides made by the otters. The snow, however, did not too often form cliffs, and so the sled provided us with most of our fun.

Before breakfast one very cold morning after a heavy rain, everything was so coated with ice that we decided that the hill from the road to Uncle Hector's home would give us a thrill. When we got to Uncle Hector's gate we were overjoyed; the hill was covered with glittering, clear ice, About a couple of hundred yards below us was the house, but the hill swept past it and on to the railroad fence, where there was a nice hollow like a small theatre into which we could steer and bank our way around to a stop. We piled onto the sled, one on top of the other, and shoved off. Almost immediately we noticed that the sled would not respond to our steering, and soon we knew we had no control at all. The sled went like the wind and made straight for Uncle Hector's kitchen door. Its aim was perfect; it struck an old, solidly frozen snow bank at the edge of the veranda, leaped high into the air, and struck right in the middle of the door. The door slammed against the wall, and we slid across the floor and on under the breakfast table, where we found ourselves mixed up with a lot of feet, some of them bare.

"Air son Dia na'n gras!" shouted Uncle Hector, calling on the God of grace; the phrase is more like a curse in Gaelic than it could be in English. "Well, of all things! Now, fellows, I am just going to give you a good skelping," said Aunt Jessie. Our beloved Aunt Jessie was always going to skelp us, but she never did. Johnnie and Neillie jumped up grumbling, Ellen and Malcolm stared at us, and Malcolm said, "We told you those kids are crazy." But it turned out as it always did; we were served breakfast of buckwheat pancakes and molasses, and tea strong enough to float a spoon. Aunt Jessie flapped her arms as she always did when agitated, and scolded us for a while, and then she was suddenly urging us to have another pancake.

We must have tried poor Aunt Jessie's soul many a time. She loved us and we loved her, but we were always having accidents that annoyed her, like sitting on the bread she had set out behind the stove, covered with a cloth, so that it would rise. We did that a number of times; she would fuss about it and then say, "Oh, I'll knead it some more and perhaps it will rise again."

One of the regrettable things about childhood is that children are never fully aware of how they love people, and so never get to tell them how they feel. One of my major feelings of guilt has come from people I greatly loved, dying before I was old enough to tell them how I loved them.

The big lake between us and Malagawatch froze over in mid-winter, and we drove over it with horse and cutter to church and to MacAuley's store. Horses were sharp-shod, and their feet made a rhythmic crunch, crunch as the calks cut into the ice. On Sundays the lake would be speckled with cutters as it was with boats in summer. We also skated almost anywhere we wanted to go when the ice was clear and smooth.

Skating was a recreation in which everyone indulged. Night was a favorite time for it, starlit or moonlit nights especially. We played a game that was faintly reminiscent of hockey, using coats for goal posts. We also had fireworks of a sort. Many cattails that grew near our shore were still intact in winter, and we would soak the cattail heads with kerosene and light them, fitting the heads into some sort of a cleft stick so that the stems wouldn't burn off too quickly; they made great showering sparks as they fell. We often skated about in procession with these torches.

The real adult sport in this season was horse-racing. Every two weeks or so during January and February fast horses would race, and everyone for many miles around came to watch; it was like Sacrament time in June. McIntyre, who kept a hotel at Orangedale, had a fast grey, a beautiful animal, that often won. For us, though, the best horse was owned by Mother's Marble Mountain cousin, Donally Mac-Donald. It had been a cart horse in the marble quarries and had been knocked down over the huge dump of rocks. The horse was such a mess by the time he reached the bottom that he was given up as valueless. Donally bought him for a couple of dollars, and made him into a race horse. He looked like a moose and ran like one. Donally cared for him with as great a love as any mother ever bestowed on a child. Donally often visited with us on his way to the races, riding on a trotting sulky—it looked like a sulky in every way except that it had runners instead of wheels. The last two or three hours before the race he would spend rubbing the horse's joints. Donally had red whiskers and a wide-open smile, with gaps between his teeth. We loved him. His horse was ugly in appearance and even uglier in motion, but it had stamina and speed.

90

I prayerfully watched him the day he took on McIntyre's grey. Donally's horse was a pacer, and rocked as though he were lame on both sides. No one ever thought that there was anything wrong in running a pacer with a trotter. He won easily.

After the races many men sought drinks at Burnt Joe's or at McIntyre's establishment. There was big talk about Big Hecky and John Eddy, the two biggest men in our neighborhood, getting into a fight at Burnt Jim's but nothing came of it. The real fracas occurred at McIntyre's, when a man we loved and admired went into action. Hughie MacDonald came from somewhere back of Whycocomagh. He was of average size, but he never lost a fight. We loved John Hughie because not only could he lick any man, but because he was a singer and a friend. He was often a guest at our home, and always sang humorous Gaelic songs, many of which were of Cape Breton origin. Mother and Father loved his singing as much as we did, and so he was always welcome and always sang. That day at Orangedale, he came out of McIntyre's dressed up like a minister except that there were tiny speckles of blood on his face and shirt front. He was grinning and dangerous, and everyone gave him room. He had just knocked out three men. It all began when someone called him a liar. The word liar was something no one could take without losing face; it was hated more than an Englishman hates having the word "bastard" applied to him. If one was called a liar he just hit out immediately without any introductory word. I was so infected with this feeling that I got into more than one squabble until I grew up and acquired some sense. I remember seeing the same behavior in an Irish film called "The Quiet Man." One could take anything from louse to "son-of-a-bitch," but one could not take being called a liar. However, the fight at McIntyre's was one that for the whole winter warmed the hearts of men who never fought themselves.

Another winter pastime was the dance at which pies were auctioned. The girls brought the pies and the buyers would be their partners for the evening. Cook and purchaser would also sit together for refreshments. Later the men would see the girls home. The dances were mostly Scottish reels and exhibitions by cloggers, but I do remember that, as I grew older, there were other folk dances and even some waltzing.

Winter had its woes, too. Towards the last of February people over fifty began to die of pneumonia and young people too now and then. Uncle Dan's oldest daughter Cathie was one. My brother John came down with it, and for days his chances weren't worth much. The house was full of people all the time; they always gathered where there was serious illness. Mother was irritated by them because of her concern for John, and Dr. Frazer MacAuley periodically told them to go home or at least to keep quiet, but they did neither. Dr. MacAuley came to see John every day, and stayed with him all night through the crisis. He was the best of doctors, although doctors of today would disapprove of the open windows in the bedroom and ice bags on John's head to keep the temperature down. There were no miracle drugs, but the doctor pulled his patient through.

There was one terrible night when Alan almost strangled with croup. Duncan had taken him for a drive in the cutter behind Dan on the ice in the cove. It was bitterly cold and they had stayed out too long. That night Alan struggled for breath so that we could hear him all over the house. That was one night when I did get down on my knees, and prayed fiercely and challengingly. The doctor was away back of Marble Mountain visiting another patient and Mother just didn't know what to do. She gave Alan almost everything she could think of and finally castor oil, although she thought it useless. Yet it did the trick; the heavy congestion gave way. I gave Mother rather than God the credit.

I never heard of any of us complaining of hunger, although we were nearly always hungry. We could have complained at times about the limited nature of our diet if we had known enough. In winter the hens stopped laying, the cows dried up, and if we had no "stripper" (a cow that hadn't been bred and so could be milked for a longer time) there was no milk at all. Black tea was an unwelcome symbol of want. The hay in the barn grew less and less so that animals were not fed as they needed to be. And yet we generally made out.

Mother could brag about never having a cow "on the lift"—that it, needing to be helped to get to her feet in the morning. All our preserved foods got used up and the last bit of butter disappeared. To have to live on brined herring, potatoes, bread and molasses was common. The potatoes gave out too if the crop had been bad or if rot infected them. There were short periods when we had little except bread and molasses, oatmeal, and tea. But really we didn't have a bad time; if we could fill our bellies with something it was enough. We used to be given cod-liver oil pretty regularly to keep off colds, and that probably helped with our diet. Anyhow our family of nine grew up. So let no one despise oatmeal, molasses, and cod-liver oil.

Probably the smelts and trout we caught now and then were more important than we realized, especially after the brined meat was gone. But real relief did not come until spring when Mother found greens such as dandelions and a weed she called lamb's quarter, and the second eel spearing began. After the ice melted and the winds drove it out of the cove, and just when the leaves began to break open the eels would be swimming freely again and they could most easily be speared at night if one had good artificial light. Colin and Alan and I would be ready with a supply of pitchy pine knots and roots which we dug mostly out of bogs. These when split and dried would burn brightly and make a fine light. Father had a firepot that could be hung out in front of the bow of a boat. In this the wood was lighted.

We sometimes accompanied the men on these eel spearing expeditions. One night Colin and I went along with Father and Peter Nicholson. They stood in front of the boat, one on each side with his spear. When an eel appeared it was speared, if one knew how to use a spear. The spears for this season were different. They had two springy hardwood jaws with a steel prod in the middle. Father hardly missed one this night. Peter missed a lot, and he blamed the spear. Father took pity on him and traded spears with him, but this made little difference in the number they caught. Once Father said, "Peter, here's a real eel. See, there with its head under the bunch of sea weed."

"Oh, man, man," said Peter, "you take it. I'll miss it for sure."

"Strike, man," father commanded, "or we'll both miss it."

Peter struck and got his eel on the spear.

"Turn your spear and let him wind himself on the pole," Father yelled. This done the big eel was brought in. It was enormous—so big that Peter's spear was broken by it. Peter, a very proud fisherman, just muttered things like, "Oh, Mother Mary," and "What a Devil-spawned thing!" and such remarks. And then he started telling about how horse-tail hair, when left in the water, could turn into eels. He could prove it. Father snorted and we giggled, and Peter argued. He had seen it happen. Father gave Peter his spear and took over the rowing which Colin and I had been doing.

It was a wonderful night. Often the smoke from the fire-pot came into our faces, and we'd have to change the direction of the boat. There were eels all about our feet. The boat seemed half filled with eels. We got home about half past two in the morning with swollen eyes and sooty faces. It was fun, great fun. It wasn't such great fun in the morning when we had to help Mother skin and clean the things, a skill which, along with all the other skills associated with eel spearing, had been learned from the Micmac Indians.

By this time cattle were in their pastures, lambs were playing and the general routine of summer was about to begin

OUR EVENING FATHER

One of my great regrets is that we didn't have coffee in
our home. Father might have been a different man at breakfast time if he had had a strong cup of coffee. I've known
coffee to accomplish miracles with domestic bears. Father
was one of those who gets up all ready to do battle whether or
not there are any enemies about, and mother served very well
as an enemy. All hell broke loose on many mornings. He'd
taste the food and it would become a target for his irritation
or he would examine his socks feverishly, looking for a place
through which he could push his little finger. I remember
once when he was looking irritably about, a newly-washed
sock fell from the drying pole above him and draped itself
across his head. We all laughed and that was enough to pre-
cipitate that morning's row. He would let out a shuddering
roar if any article of clothing he needed was not within his
reach. We children would all line up along the wall, not saying anything but obviously supporting Mother, and that made
him wilder than ever. When he was ready to go to work he
would examine his lunch and if he could find no fault he
would slam out the door, walk a couple of steps, and then

come back and tell us more about how everyone was persecuting him. Mother knew very well that he had to be treated as gingerly as a king cobra, but she couldn't resist hitting back by hinting how things might be better if he attended to his responsibilities as he should. God knows, she had provocation enough. She would have had to be both a pacifist and a person of monumental strength to do all she did and on top of that to treat him as though he were a bit of precious crystal. He just had to provoke someone and he could have provoked the angel Gabriel. A sense of peace would flood the place when he really and finally shut the door. Nothing would be said, but Mother would weep. These morning fights were the only things about my home that I was ashamed of; I was always fearful that others might hear about them. Fathers and mothers who fought were not in high repute with children. We knew about every couple who habitually had spats; it was almost as bad as having a bastard in the family.

If our morning father was hard to understand, our evening father was quite impossible to explain, for we never had any desire to judge him. He was entirely and completely acceptable. We would run to meet him as he returned from his day's heavy labor, go through his lunch pail for leftovers, ride him piggyback, and barrage him with questions. He always had time for us then; he played games with us or did stunts like standing on his head on a fence post, and was generally good for a story. He had no kinship whatever with the "snarliyow" of the morning.

He taught us all sorts of tricks, such as how to climb up a doorway by pressing with hands and feet against the casings until we reached the top, when we would hook our fingertips over the inch-thick casing above the swing free, "skinning the cat" several times. He taught us one trick with a chair. It was set down with its front legs lying on the floor and its back on the upperside. Then someone would mount it, his toes on the lowest rung and his hands grasping the lower parts of the back side-posts. Then he would tip the chair down so that the top of the back would reach the floor, pushing his backside away back so that it would go down gently. Then he would take all his weight on his arms and go down head first and pick something—a thimble, for instance—from the floor with his mouth, and then rise and return the chair to its original position without falling off the chair.

There was also a trick with a broom. Someone would set the end of the broom handle perpendicularly against the floor, then turn out his feet and legs, and lower himself until one hand was within an inch of the floor. Then he would swing his body under his lower arm and come up on the other side to a standing position. We had many a hilarious time after supper doing things like that.

If Father was not in the mood for such calisthenics, he was generally good for a story, although his stories were not of the nicey-nice kind. They had been orally transmitted and must have been very old indeed, for they had all the primitive earmarks. There was never any hint of sexual obscenity about them, but they had everything else. Most of them were about the exploits of a hero whom he called "Donald the Hero," or something that sounded like that. Donald behaved like an impishly clever child.

I can only give a sample or two. Donald was, as usual, looking for adventure when he chanced upon a slaughter-house. There was nothing interesting about it, but he did pick up a pocketful of pigs' tails that he thought might be useful sometime. He stopped to pester a witchwoman by throwing pebbles from behind some cover at her disreputable abode until she screamed with rage. Satisfied with that, he moved on, and soon came to the sea, where he found a beautiful beach with some quicksand nearby. On the hill above him people were working in their fields, and there were some pigs just below the brow of the hill. At once he had an idea. He drove the pigs out of sight and stuck his pigs' tails in the edge of the quicksand, just far enough so that they stood up nicely. Then he raised a great clamor, shouting to the people on the hill that their pigs had sunk into the quicksand. All the people rushed to the shore, and each grabbed a pig's tail and pulled. When they saw they had been tricked they rushed for Donald and might have killed him if he hadn't jumped into their one and only boat and pushed off from shore, leaving the people cursing him helplessly. He dared not return to the beach and so rowed away towards the sea. He hadn't gone far before he noticed a wooded island in the distance and steered for that. It was a long row, and he was glad indeed when he finally beached the boat and wandered into the forest, alert once more for something unusual. Suddenly he was startled by a great roar and a loud thrashing in the woods. It occurred to him then that this must be the island on which the famous monster lived, the monster who devoured anyone who trespassed on his private domain. Donald at once selected a big tree, climbed into it, and hid in its branches. It wasn't long before he heard the monster approaching, sniffing loudly; apparently the monster had scented him. Soon the monster was at the base of the tree, pounding on the trunk.

"Who's oop thar?" he bellowed.

"God," said Donald.

"Proof it!" demanded the monster.

"I'll throw you oop a rock and you turn it into water. That should be easy for you, if it's God himself that you are."

"Throw the rock," said Donald.

The rock came crashing through the branches and Donald deftly caught it, put it into his pocket, and then peed down on the monster.

"Indit it's God himself that you are," said the monster; "I am honored. Coom down and be guest at my house."

Donald came down and the monster escorted him to his home, which was surrounded with human bones, and there Donald was generously provided with food. In the evening he was shown to a room in which was an enormous bed. The monster bade him goodnight with an evil gleam in his eye, saying the bed was so comfortable that he might sleep in it forever.

He was no sooner gone than Donald was out of bed again. He made a dummy man from things he found in the room, put it in the bed, and covered it as though it were a person. Then he crawled underneath the bed for a nice nap.

In the middle of the night he was awakened by the monster, who was trying to tiptoe quietly into the room. He carried an enormous cudgel with which he belabored the dummy until it was thoroughly flattened out. As he left the room he said triumphantly, "God or no God, that should do for you."

Donald slept until morning, and then went out to join his host, who was more than amazed to see him. Sometime later the monster put a huge caldron on the fire, into which he put a whole pig, announcing that he was about to make a soup worthy of his honored guest. Donald thanked him and said that he was particularly fond of soup; in fact, that he was a champion soup eater whom no mortal could equal. The monster took him on at once and said that he could eat as much soup as any God, again with the vicious gleam in his eye.

So it was the soup was prepared, but while the monster was cooking it Donald found a pigskin that had been sewn up for carrying water, and it gave him an idea. He pushed the pigskin down under his clothes with the opening just under his chin.

When the contest began Donald spooned most of his soup into the pigskin, just swallowing some occasionally whenever the monster looked his way. They were getting close to the end of the soup when Donald stretched, sighed, took his knife, and stuck himself in the belly (really the pigskin), and the soup gushed out. "Oh, that's a great relief," he said, sighing comfortably. The monster was not to be outdone, and so he too stuck himself in the belly, and the soup he had eaten ran out. And that was the end of the monster.

Most of Father's stories had something in them that would take courage even to print today. Another such story was the one about the man who drank his fill from a brook, went upstream a bit, and found the brook running right through a dead dog from one end to the other as though the dog were drinking and evacuating it all at once. The thought of impropriety never entered our heads, nor his either. References to excreta were funny, not improper. Those stories contributed much to the good father-son relationship among us —in the evenings, that is. A few can be told without editing.

99

There were innumerable tales about the escapades in which Donald always proved himself to be the hero. Robbers, pirates, and even kings could not get the best of him.

In addition to Donald's exploits, Father had a store of bear stories. In our time there were no bear in Cape Breton but there had been a lot when Father was a boy. We wished they would come back again. The next best thing was to get Father to tell about Ewan Mohr and his bear hunting. So one night when he was relaxing on the couch, smoking his pipe, we asked him to tell one of the stories.

This is the story:- "When Ewan was young there were many bears and he had more than his share living on his property. One night they stole three sheep. That was when he decided to make war on them. The leader of the pack was a huge one eyed bear that Ewan thought he had wounded many years ago. He spent a day making lead bullets, and walked from Little Harbor where he lived, to MacAuley's store at Malagawatch to get a supply of powder. When he got home he took down the old flint-lock from where it hung on the wall and began to load it. For wadding he used bits of cotton cloth, moss or paper.

"It did not take him long to find the bear tracks, and he could plainly see where the sheep had been dragged away. Following the trail he found a half eaten sheep partly covered with leaves, left there for another meal. He sat there for hours, so it seemed. Suddenly a squirrel went "twrrrrrrrrrrrr" close to his head. He nearly jumped out of his skin. Before he could get his breath he saw the big bear coming slowly, raising his snout into the wind, sniffing. He began to uncover the sheep and to eat greedily. Ewan took careful aim at the top of the bear's head and pulled the trigger. The bear let out a growly squeal, shook his head and came for Ewan. He must have had a skull of iron, Ewan thought. Ewan had no time to reload his muzzel-loading musket, so he climbed into a maple tree where he began to reload. By the time he had pushed the bullet down with his ramrod and the wadding after it, the big bear was half way up the tree. This time Ewan shot him right through the head, and he crashed to the ground like a sack of rocks. Ewan could see other bears around him as he reloaded.

100

He decided that the best place to be was home. He dropped to the ground and ran, but immediately another bear rose upon his hind legs, right in his path. He shot that one and quickly made for another tree which he climbed and began to reload as fast as he could. He could see bear all over the place and before he had finished loading the gun a third one pulled off his leather legging. He shot that bear, and then came down, running like mad to make another tree. He hadn't taken more than a dozen steps when a "boxing bear" knocked him flying. When he got up he grabbed the beast by the cheeks and kicked him in the stomach with his one boot. The bear backed away and he grabbed his gun and ran. He climbed a tree again reloaded and shot two more bears before he came down. When he reached ground once more another bear was on top of him knocking the musket out of his hands. It flew in the air, fell on a stump and went off, killing two more bear.

Alan and Colin and I looked at each other. We knew this was a whopper but Father went on. "He killed nine bears that day," he concluded.

We egged him on to telling the Donald Cameron story.

Donald was eleven years old the day he went to have a look at his father's bear trap, and he found a big bear caught in it by a hind foot. Donald had no business being there, but it was a thrill to see the bear. The chain that held the trap to a stump was too long, and the bear got to him in one jump, knocked him flat, jumped on top of him, and opened its ugly mouth to grab him by the throat. Donald instinctively grabbed the bear by the root of its tongue, dug his fingers into it, and hung on for dear life, so that the bear couldn't clamp down on his hands with its teeth. The bear made terrifying yelling sounds, which was a good thing, for a neighbor heard the racket and came and shot it.

We suspected that one was a whopper too, but we couldn't be sure because we didn't think anyone could think of grabbing the bear's tongue unless it was true. Some stories we knew were true, like the one about "Murdoch the Bear."

Murdoch was following a woods road long after dark. His feet seemed to find the way even though he was quite drunk; he had been to a party of some sort at "Light Archie's." He swayed back and forth as he walked, but he felt like the strongest man in the world. Then he thought he saw something against a bit of sky. He stopped to make sure, and after a little he saw a bear coming along the road to meet him. Murdoch picked up a big stick and felt all his muscles rippling. The bear acted as if he wanted to keep politely to its own side of the road, but Murdoch was not quite so polite. He went for the bear and struck him a fearful blow on the head with the club he had picked up. The bear reared up, struck the club out of Murdoch's hands, grabbed him around the shoulders, and bit the skin and hair right off the top of his head. Someone else going home from the same party found him nearly dead from loss of blood. Murdoch was tough and recovered, but he always had a shiny bald spot, and after that he was known as "Murdoch the Bear."

There were stories about other animals, too. My grandmother MacRae shot a seal once, and a great uncle who was a sailor boarded a whale he thought was dead, and had what was probably one of the first submarine rides anyone ever had.

Father loved to tell about the big cat he once shot, which was always a mystery to him. No one who had not seen it would believe that there had ever been such an animal. This story was no whopper; we knew by the way Father talked when he was telling the truth. He had a little terrier dog, and one morning before breakfast the terrier set up a shattering howl and was off as though the devil himself were after him. Mother looked out the window—this was when they lived in the cabin on the hill—and much to her astonishment she saw an enormous animal that looked like a cat although it seemed as big as a colt, walking across the cleared field by the cabin in the direction of the river. When it saw the dog it made off with great graceful leaps, and both cat and dog soon disappeared over the bank of the river. Father got into his clothes, grabbed his gun, and followed the dog's barking upstream until he caught up with them. The dog was by then so excited that his voice slivered into little squeaks; he had the cat treed in a big pine. The first shot brought the cat down, and the dog grabbed it by the ear and tried to shake it—it was his prize and he wanted everyone to know it.

The only wild cat known in Cape Breton was the bobcat, and this one would make a dozen bobcats. The bobcat is gray and has a stub of a tail, but this animal was brown and had a very long tail. Father never found out what the animal was, but years later I saw a puma in British Columbia and it fitted father's description perfectly. Some think pumas (also called cougar and mountain lion), were once spread all over the continent, but this big cat remained a mystery, for no one who did not see the animal could believe the story.

This father of ours, this gymnast and story teller, had no kinship with the bearish man we knew at breakfast-time, and we never got the two confused. A man we did not like threw his weight around in the morning, but quite a different person came home in the evening.

Mother, too, had her moments when worry left her. There were times when the work got done, and she sat at the spinning-wheel and sang as she kept it humming. She had a beautiful voice and knew many old Gaelic songs. The spinning-wheel was her piano and the spinning chore her relaxing time, except when someone dropped in for a "ceilidh" (a friendly visit). The great brown earthenware teapot was always on the back of the stove. When someone called, she'd put it on to heat, adding more tea and more hot water. She served bread and butter, and maybe preserved fruit, with the tea.

Mother did all the spanking in the family, but I don't remember any of us retaining any resentment about it. Father never touched us, even in the mornings, except once when we drove him beyond his control. We got to giggling at the table, and after three warnings from him, one of us guffawed, spraying food all over the table. Father reached each of us with the

103

back of his hand, and it felt like Samson's jawbone. We saw stars and immediately left the table, filled with a great sense of injury. In about fifteen minutes or so I walked around the far end of the barn just as Alan was turning towards me from the opposite corner. We sidled up to each other without a word, still sulking. After a while I sneaked a look at him just as he looked at me, and he said through the corner of his mouth, "Damn good enough for us,"—and so it was.

THE INVASION

We gave little attention to the middle-aged man who took soil borings from our back pastures and from Uncle Hector's fields, but a year later we did notice, for Uncle Hector sold his place to a brick-making concern. The man who had done borings was in charge, a Mr. Lantz. Things moved quickly, and in a few weeks the part of Uncle Hector's farm next to the cove was filled with carts and scrapers, a siding or spur from the railway was built, and before long carloads of gear, dozens of great beautiful horses and feed were unloaded. A three-story building to house the workers was built, and it looked like a castle to us. A whole colony of sheds for brick drying was erected, and plows and scrapers soon got busy at removing the topsoil and laying bare the heavy deposit of red clay from which the bricks were to be made.

Winter set in before any brick-making could be done, and the workmen were sent in to the woods along with many local people to cut cordwood for heating the kilns. Father, who was now in his sixties, resigned his railway job, a move that frightened mother almost out of her wits, and along with John and Neil, began slashing trees and cutting them into

105

four-foot lengths for the brickworks. It was an excellent opportunity to profitably use up the half-grown timber that bordered our pastures, and Lantz's big horses hauled the sticks away on enormous bobsleds; besides, father sold the stumpage on some of the wood to Lantz and his chopping crews. A team of those big horses could haul a full cord—a pile eight feet by four—in one load.

After school and on Saturdays we rode back and forth on the loads of cord wood, but most of our time was spent helping Father and John and Neil pile their cuttings, a cord in each pile. Mother was happy over the situation. At the noon hour she fed not only her own three working men but a half a dozen others. Duncan brought her a dinner horn with which she called the men to lunch, and the blasts she gave on it were happy and cheerful. She tried to keep away her fear of the future, when there would be no jobs or when the brickyard closed down; and especially she tried to fight off the fear that the farm might not legally be in our possession any longer. Mother's worry was not entirely irrational; some cash income was needed to buy necessities that could not be manufactured at home. The loom was no longer used for any fabric except blanket material, and so clothes had to be bought. There was also sugar, molasses, oatmeal, and cornmeal—in fact, quite a number of things. Shoes for everybody was a big item; Father no longer made shoes. His cash income from the railway job had been little enough, but now that he thought he had to retire, where was our money to come from? Mother often had to deny us eggs and butter so that she could add something to our credit at the store. John had often contributed his earnings to the family, but he could not be expected to continue doing so. Neil was a restless sort who never stayed too long on a job. At this time he was planning to save for a trip to Mexico, where he was told he could get a job in a gold mine. Duncan at fifteen had lied his way into a job as a brakeman on the I.C.R. (Intercolonial Railway); he would have to support himself and couldn't be expected to save much for a while. The real source of worry for Mother was that everything we sold—eggs, butter, lumber, etc.—all went to merchant Dan in Orangedale, what we needed was charged against what we gave, and for years Father hadn't had an ac-

106

counting to find out where he stood. Mother didn't need an overactive imagination to fear that all the property we had was in jeopardy, and she half expected that merchant Dan would foreclose at any moment and leave us with nothing at all. Merchants had gathered in a lot of farms that way. She constantly badgered and pestered Father to get an accounting, but although he reassured her he would, he had never gotten around to it and so she lived in fear. While the wood-cutting lasted it would be better than the railway job, but how long would it last? And how long would the brick business last?

The Gaelic community was now shattered. The men Lantz had brought in were of many kinds and included a number of Frenchmen. The province, even the Cape Breton end of it, had pockets of very old French communities here and there whose forebears had been among the first to settle on the continent. Their ways, their speech, and their manners generally were alien to us, and it became necessary for us to use the Gaelic only when we were alone together. Mother had to try to speak English, which annoyed her a great deal; her English was, to say the least, rudimentary. We thought she was terribly slow to pick it up and often laughed at her efforts, although our own grammer was a long way from perfect. In contrast, her sister, Aunt Mary, had spent many years in Boston, where she became so fluent in the "Sassenach" tongue that she refused to teach Gaelic to her children. Mother thought Mary was looking down her beautiful long nose at her. Aunt Jessie's English was just as meager as Mother's, and even her Gaelic was unusual. Her people had been MacLeods from Lewis, who transmitted their accent to Jessie.

One day a French boy came to the house and tried to tell Mother something in English that was even poorer than her own, and failing, he switched to French. Mother threw up her hands and responded in Gaelic, "If you are going to talk in that language I'll talk in my own," she said. "After all, I've heard it said that Gaelic was the language of Eden, and that if you don't speak a word of Gaelic at all you're not going to find it easy to get into Heaven." There was a twinkle in her eye, the boy laughed and switched to sign language, and in that ancient and universal medium of communication they got along very well.

107

Another consequence of the invasion was the need for locks. Father's entire stock of brined meat was stolen in one night, and he was so shocked at the theft that he seemed in a stupor for days.

Our religion also suffered a loss about this time. People went to church as usual, but they went for vigorous preaching rather than for the word. There was also an increase in evangelistic appeals.

The brickworks were too far away from any place that could provide workmen with any kind of diversion, and so we had scads of company almost every evening. Jim Fraunk and Norman Ross (who later married my sister Mary) and a half a dozen others were nearly always down at our house in the evenings. We had more dances than any one home should have had, but there were the men and the neighboring girls, my sisters were old enough by then to dance, and there was Johnnie Hector who, by some strange magic of heredity, had become a virtuoso on the violin. Brother Neil could play jigs very well, but he was so outclassed by Johnnie that he was shy of touching the instrument while Johnnie was around. Johnnie would listen to a hornpipe from our Edison cylinder records, and a day or two later could play it so that we couldn't tell it from the original. Under such circumstances dancing was inevitable. They mostly did Scottish reels, especially the foursome and eightsome. When anyone was present who could clog he was given lots of opportunity to wear out his shoes and the floors. How often I was sent to bed in great sadness before the glorious racket subsided. Any excuse at all, such as a birthday or a holiday would do for a dance; they would have danced at a funeral if someone had suggested it.

The dancing and occasional drinking didn't improve our status as church-people, but there were enough sinners about to provide us with good company, although such behavior could have serious consequences for some people. About the time I left home a group of teenagers (communicants) had their names stricken from the church roles for attending a dance en masse.

There was a memorable shakedown after a fulling bee. Mother had had a weaver (a "kicker" in Gaelic) come to the house for a few days, who wove many yards of blankets, and so the fulling bee was held. A row of low tables had been put together out of planking and strung around the parlor, which was very rarely used, and everyone sat behind them. The moistened blanketing was stretched along the tables around the room. There was music and a song with a good beat, and everyone sang, grasping the blanketing and pounding it against the table in time with the music. After a certain number of beats the blanketing was shoved on counter-clockwise, and so the material went around and around the room until it was properly fluffed. Then drinks were served: Scotch, taken straight. One brickyard man wanted water with it, and we regarded him as a weakling. Then the dancing began and continued until the small hours of the morning.

From Christmas through New Year's there was drinking. For the brickmen it was continuous; they ordered cases of whiskey from Kelley and Glassey in Halifax. It was no surprise for us to find the empty packing cases in the barn, and now and then a man or two stretched out dead to the world on the barn floor. One night when a crowd of men were in the house, Mother and I went on some errand to the barn and found Danny Murdoch snoring off his first drink. He was just fifteen years old. Mother forgot her errand, marched back to the house, and gave the assembled merry-makers the sharp edge of her tongue. She told them, along with a number of other things, that they were welcome at our home but that they would not be if they took advantage of another youngster and she found out about it.

Father was a likeable host and very generous in his judgment of men who drink, as long as they stayed on their feet. When someone brought a bottle into the house, Father would drink with superb dignity and brag about never having been put off his feet by liquor. I never saw him even sway or swagger, but he would become so affable that he would roar with laughter at almost anything, and would stamp his feet as he sat in his chair and talked. We were a bit ashamed of him when he got that way. Mother would take a drink with the men, but rarely a second one. She was a gracious hostess no matter what the company, and people loved her just as much as they regarded Father as the best of fellows.

When a very special guest joined us at the table, Father would bring out his special bottle. Everybody, even the youngest of us, would have to take a sip in honor of the guest, and he never let such a guest leave without a "doch an dores" (the parting drink at the door). We didn't like the taste, but it was a family ritual and we dared not refuse.

Once after Christmas in this first year with the brickmen, when everyone was away except we three boys and Flora, we gathered dozens of whiskey bottles from about the barn and drained the few drops each contained into one bottle. Colin was for drinking it, but when he tasted it he made a face, and we decided that the thing to do was to give it to our dog Purdy. We soaked a big piece of bread with the stuff and set it down on the floor, and Purdy gulped it down with great relish. We poured what was left on another slice and he gulped that down and furiously barked for more. In a minute or two he began to froth at the mouth and to run about in great excitement. Then he reared up at a window, looked out, and began to growl furiously. There was nothing outside to growl at, and we concluded that he was seeing things. When someone said that maybe he had what the men called the D.T.'s, we took fright. Flora started for the stairs, and soon we were all racing for the attic, with Purdy at our heels. There was a hatch door to the entrance to the attic, and we barely made it through in time to slam the door down in Purdy's face. We didn't come down until Mother and Father returned, and by that time Purdy was sober.

About the time winter broke up, Mr. Lantz died of pneumonia, a brother of his took over the business, and whatever plans the first Mr. Lantz had in mind were discarded. The drying-sheds were torn down, and a huge, old-fashioned kiln shed was built. Then the making of bricks began.

Water was needed and so the dam of the old mill was repaired enough to provide a sufficient head of water, and a pipeline was laid down to the point on the shoreline nearest the brickworks. There a hill had to be crossed, and so they

110

built a tank thirty feet in the air and pumped the water into it; from there the water flowed to the machines. Uncle Dan's oldest boy, Johnnie, did the work with a hand pump. He was little more than a boy, but he kept the tank as full as any man could.

My brother John was given a job, and I often watched him and other men work the machines. A horse provided the power; hitched to a long pole eight or nine feet from the ground, he went around and around the machine, and so mixed the clay, water, and sand. A man would pull down a lever vigorously and then remove a tray at the bottom of the machine that contained six, or maybe four, new wet bricks; then he would run out on a smooth court, deftly turn the tray, deposit the bricks gently on the ground, and run back for more. There were three machines operating in that way. The men worked in their bare feet and generally sang some kind of silly song as they ran. We kids picked up a lot of shamelessly obscene ditties which no doubt added something to our education.

When the bricks were dried enough in the sun to be handled, they were transported to the kiln. The packing was something to see. The bricks were stacked so that the heat could easily reach them, and tunnels ran in gothic style at the base from one side of the mammoth brick-pile to the other. The tunnels were for the fires. When the brick pile became ten feet or more in height the bricks were thrown, four at a time, to a man at the top who caught them more easily than if they had been handed to him. The bricks never separated on their way up, and I never tired of watching the dexterity of those men. John was usually the man at the top. Before long the pile was complete and the firing began. Fires were started at the entrances of the tunnels, and then, as the four-foot sticks burned, wood was thrown more and more deeply into the tunnels until the fires burned from side to side. A man stoked constantly, night and day. I stayed up half one night with a stoker, fascinated by the fires in the quiet night.

When the bricks were thoroughly cured, box-cars were pushed onto the siding and loading for shipment began. There was nothing exciting about it except one day when a boxcar got derailed and the wrecking train came to pull it back on the track. They used a rope that looked six inches in diameter, and yet when the strain came on it, it looked like twine. The engine didn't dare go very far on the siding.

It rather surprises men that I can't recall any fights among the brickmen; at least there were none that we ever heard about. Only once we were aware of bad feeling between any of the men, and that was between Jim Fraunk and Ted Mooney, both of whom were teamsters. Jim had a great love for his horses. They always looked as though they were waxed and polished, and their tails and manes would have done credit to a professional hairdresser. Their harnesses were oiled, bespangled with decorative brass that glittered in the sun; rosettes of many colors decorated the bridles. Mooney was hired at the brickworks later than Jim and was a thoroughly good teamster who offered Jim stiff competition. Before long he began to hint about something being wrong but would not say what. Sitting on the porch with us after dinner, he told us of shoes pulled from his horses' feet, harness cut, animals turned loose at night, and ornaments stolen. What had finally moved him to talk was the discovery that someone had greased the insides of his horses' mouths so that they would not eat. He was worried and angry and suspected Jim, who had a jealous enough nature to resent another teamster, but we could not credit him with taking out his spite on those beautiful animals. The two men finally got into a terrible row in front of Uncle Hector's old carriage shop, yelling so loudly at each other that we could hear almost every word clear back at our home; Ted had apparently laid his charges on the line. The two men didn't come to blows, but somehow the row ended the molesting of the animals.

The brick business brought us youngsters a new chore. we had three pigs to fed, and the Lantz cook-house provided us with lots of garbage which we collected every morning. We soon discovered that the cook prepared food for only one meal at a time and had no use for leftovers, dumping anything the man didn't eat—hunks of meat, whole vegetables, and leftover cake, fancier food by far than we ate most of the time, making us jealous of our gourmet porkers. One day the cook called us back after we started for home and dumped a whole baker's sheet of fresh cookies into the pail. There they lay, on top of the clean paper that covered the garbage. We argued ourselves into regarding the cookies as thoroughly sanitary and ate the whole batch before we got home.

One morning the cook gave me a new jackknife. He took it from his pocket, opened it, and stuck it into the wall by my ear, saying it was "bad luck to give anyone a gift of a sharp-pointed instrument; but there it is in the wall, and if anyone takes it, it will not be as though I had given it to him." I took it, thinking he was pretty stupid to have such notions. Then I began to suspect that the clean paper which he had so carefully tucked over the garbage was put there with the cookies in mind. Maybe he had a superstition about giving away cookies too.

There was another invasion brought by the coming of the brick men. One night Mother came up from the cellar with the news that she had seen a rat in the potato bin. There hadn't been a rat near our home for years. I had never seen one, but there were many of them when our parents were young. Now they had returned with the horse-feed.

There were many animals on the Nova Scotia mainland that, in so far as we knew, weren't in Cape Breton at all; such as bear, moose, deer, woodchucks, skunks, and porcupines. There had been many bears during Father's boyhood and probably some of the other creatures as well. But why did they leave? Plague? Forest fires? No one seemed to know. There must have been rats, although we had escaped them locally. Deer were brought in later and flourished, and now any creature can walk across the causeway over the Strait of Canso.

The night of Mother's announcement Colin and Alan and I were interested enough to go into the cellar with a feeble light and sit still for an hour or more before we saw Mother's rat. We thought it was nothing to get excited about but we were to know better later.

Colin and I were sent to the barn to flail—that is, to thresh the oats—and we found the grain pretty well threshed already, and the straw badly chopped up, and rat runways visible all through the haymows. In a very short time the oat crop was a total loss. When one walked into the big unloading room with a light at night there would be hundreds of rats scurrying and fighting with each other to get down a hole in one corner of the room. The pigs were molested too. Looking through a knot hole after "slopping" the pigs, one could see their feeding troughs so full of rats that the pigs would back away and let them have the feed.

We declared war but we were not equipped for it. Father bought a trap that caught a rat every night, but, as he said, for every one he caught a dozen came to its funeral. I set out all our muskrat traps, and every time I visited the trap there would be a rat in it, yet the rats increased in number. In the spring they killed and ate Mother's newly-hatched chicks. Mother also had a brood of ducklings which she kept in an old grain box at night. Yet when half grown they were all killed one night. Several big, gaping holes in the heavy lumber of the box told the tragic story.

I tried everything on them—shot gun, snares, and even fishhooks. I set a baited fishhook in a hole one evening and in the morning found one of Mother's prize egg-layers in great distress, flying about tethered to a fishline. Mother was very angry, not merely about the prize hen, but about the cruelty of my hunting methods. John did some expert surgery, filing off the hook after he had pulled the poor bird's crop into its mouth. The joke of it was that the chicken broke all egg-laying records the following year. Father laughed and said, "Just like people. Some of them need a barb in their crops." Father took a hand in the war on the rats, setting out a barrel half full of water and carefully covering the water with light chaff. He drowned dozens of rats, but they finally learned to keep away from the barrel. When the snow left us John's old muzzle-loading gun became the best weapon. I'd load it with just two or three BB pellets and then lie on the grass and watch where the rats had run from a hole in the barn foundation to the pigpen. I could shoot a rat and be reloaded about the time the next one ventured out. Although this was great sport it

114

did not stem the rising tide of rats. Nothing stopped them until we gave them a mammoth dose of poison. We set it out in a small room that the other animals could not get into, and in the morning there were many dead rats about; not a living one could be seen, and they did not appear again. Uncle Dan complained a few days later, saying we had driven the rats to his place. They will sometimes all leave that way when poisoned. Anyhow, Uncle Dan also used poison, and the war was won.

For two summers a great many bricks were made and shipped, and then the business closed down, and for good. Afterwards, Father looked after the buildings and other properties and sold off the furnishings, the tools and the remaining bricks for Mr. Lantz. Father was then without income of any sort, and mother's worries returned with a vengeance. But he was always busy. He began to feel compelled to build fences and then to move them about to make new patterns of fields. He made himself a set of bobsleds after the design of the ones the brick people used, and did a beautiful job. He also built a fine addition to the barn. First he hewed all the logs and cut and bored them, so that they were all ready to be erected and put together. Then he called on the neighbors, and the building went up in a day, with everything falling into place. He was always making beautifully polished axe handles and giving them away. Every evening he would whittle on them with a crooked knife of Micmac design, leaving shavings, bits of glass, and sandpaper around his chair. Every neighbor wanted a handle, and Father charged them nothing at all, with the result that Mother was irritated because this activity contributed nothing to the family budget. Then one day he surprised us by taking us to the woods with cross-cut saw and axes and we began to cut timber for the coal industry at Sydney Mines. This was thenceforth our main source of income. Everything was turned over to merchant Dan for marketing, and the status of the family on merchant Dan's books was still unknown.

MOTHER HAS HER DAY

Once a visiting minister preached on the text: "There-fore take no thought, saying, what shall we eat, or what shall we drink? or, wherewithall shall we be clothed? . . . for your heavenly Father knoweth that ye need all these things." This was the one and only subject on which Mother seemed to resent the teaching of the church. The philosophy implicit in her behavior was "Root, hog, or die." She would never have used such a challenging slogan as that, but it worried her deeply to be told that she had no need to worry and scheme for tomorrow, and work herself sick to keep the household going. Her response to the sermon was, "If God knows what we need and supplies us with what we deserve, then we have no hope at all. I'd like to see this family picking up its food and clothing like the birds of the air!" She generally worked as though she were facing a crisis, and some of her feeling, probably more than we were aware of, got home to us.

While Father was a railway section boss he did very little at home except to help us with the wood-cutting now and then. He often spent hours after work in leisure, while

116

Mother flitted about on one errand after another, and that was the reason why he was such a wonderful father to us in the evenings after his day's work was done. I think Mother appreciated the good place he had in our lives in the evenings, for she expressed no resentment over the time he spent in play with us.

After he resigned from the railway and the brick business closed down, we often joined him in work as well as play. He liked to have us with him when he worked, perhaps because he liked to teach us. When we first joined him in the woods he felled the bigger trees while Colin and I "junked" them into the required lengths, which mostly made what we called pit props.

We also limbed trees. When a tree was big enough for a fourteen foot log or two, Father would measure out the logs, leaving us to do the sawing and the cutting of the tops into pit props. Alan was privileged to snake out the logs with our horse Gordon. Gordon knew what to do and didn't need much driving. Alan attached the toting chain to the logs, hooked Gordon to them, and told him to go and the horse would take them to the pile by the road, where he would wait for his teamster. Father took advantage of every opportunity to teach us without appearing to make a point of teaching.

He loved problems for the teaching opportunities they brought. Once we forgot to bring the chain, and he expressed concern. Then he stood, legs wide apart, and asked, "What are we going to do now? It's too late and too far back home to go there and back. I've never been stuck yet, but this problem looks like a dandy." Then he searched in the scrub, and came back with a handful of slender switches. "Let's see what we can do with these bits of black willow," he said. Putting one end of a switch under his foot, he twisted and twisted each switch until it was thoroughly limber from end to end. Then he tied the switches together and knotted them about the end of a log. "Now, Gordon," he said, "away with you!" And as Gordon dragged the log away, Father's "Aha" was a shout of triumph.

Another time, when making railway ties, he forgot to bring the blue chalk for the striking line to mark the sticks for hewing. He seemed distressed for a while, and then said, "Now I wonder." He started a little fire, and, when it was reduced to hot coals, built an ovenlike enclosure around it of rocks and moss, threw two pieces of a pine limb onto the coals, and sealed the whole thing up. "Now let's go on to something else while that is cooking. I can do the hewing later," he said. After a while he kicked the oven apart and displayed two sticks of charcoal, which, when he had stripped some bark from a log, served to chalk a line very well.

He instructed us in safety precautions when necessary. "Angus, if you mean to fell that tree first, make a notch in the exact direction in which you want the tree to fall. Then chop away on the opposite side, making the cut parallel to the notch. And look about you for any limbs or twigs that might catch your axe. Did I ever tell you about the time old Donald Ban went to work in the lumber woods in Pennsylvania? There was a witch-woman there who claimed that, for a fee, she could keep the men from cutting themselves. No one who went to her would tell what she had said. Donald was curious about her and half believed she had unnatural powers. So he went to see her, and she charged him fifty cents, a whole day's wage, which he had to pay before she told him anything. Do you know what she told him? 'When you are about to fell a tree or to use your axe for any purpose, look about you and take careful note of every twig or limb that may be in the path of your axe when you swing it. Remove them all before cutting your tree, and you'll come out of the woods with a whole skin and still in possession of all your toes.' That's all she gave him for his good money, the old bitch, as if he didn't already know about such things; but she was right, damn her devil-possessed soul, she was right."

Alan wanted to know why he always had to drag out the logs small end first. "Easier and safer that way," said Father, and then hitched the horse to the butt end of the log and let us watch the log dig into the earth, hook onto trees and stumps, and roll and switch its small end about in a way that would break people's legs.

118

The timber that we cut was hauled to a siding close by the old schoolhouse and was there loaded onto railway cars for shipment. Every stick was credited to merchant Dan, who marketed them. We never knew what the mining company paid for them or what credit was given against our purchases at Dan's store, and neither did Father. This marketing system was typical of many parts of the province until, many years after we left home, the system was broken up by the cooperative movement. Lumber, fish, and anything else we produced went to merchant Dan and he set the price both on what he bought and what he sold. Our situation was not improved by Father's reluctance to find out what our debt or credit was; his only justifying argument was to say that "Merchant Dan is an honest man."

When Father was busy with fish nets, sowing seed, or moving fences about, we worked in the bush by ourselves. The year I was thirteen we cut and loaded three carloads of pit props by ourselves. It was no great year's work, but not bad considering everything. During most of that winter proper footwear was a special problem. I wore an old pair of rubber boots that "Begod" our perennial guest had discarded. They froze as hard as rocks with the toes turned straight up, and, although they reached to my crotch, the snow usually got into them. Colin had only shoes and suffered greatly from cold feet. Alan had the best equipment, a pair of home-made cloth moccasins, called "moccan" in Gaelic. The "moccan" were made of many layers of cloth sewed onto old socks until they were quite thick; in the dry snow of midwinter there was nothing better. Of course, whenever we got them wet, we had to go home for a fresh pair or get our feet frozen. The moccan also had the disadvantage of being impossible to clean once they got dirty, and it didn't take long to get them dirty.

We, the young fry, never had any money at all unless we earned it in some special way of our own; only once were we paid for necessary work around the home, when Father promised us twenty-five cents if we cut up all the stove wood in a pile that the horses had hauled in. We would have cut most of it anyhow, but the short time in which we did the job was worth something. Colin and Alan were each given a twenty-five cent piece, but my coin turned out to be just a twenty cent piece, although Father probably hadn't noticed the difference in the coins. My effort to remedy the mistake was not successful.

Once I found a dollar bill on the railroad track as we were coming back from school, and I could hardly believe my eyes. All three of us jumped and shouted with joy as we ran for home—we were rich! We had great discussions about what we should buy with the money, but we were finally persuaded by Mother and the girls to buy some blue denim with which to make our pants, and that's what happened to my first great fortune.

Another time I found a two-dollar bill in the yard at home. One of the Lantz boys must have dropped it, but we could not find the owner, and so I went to the clock where Mother kept her treasures. The spending of it was something to dream about. Then one day I returned from school and found Mother very unhappy. She told me that the man who collected money for the minister had come and found her without a penny. We had contributed nothing the year before; she had to find something for him, and so the two dollar bill became an offering to the Lord. Mother asked me if I could think of anything else she could have done, and I couldn't. Nevertheless, I resented that gift so much that it is a wonder I ever studied for the ministry. I was also perplexed by the fact that an act can be justified and still be wrong. I turned to hunting.

It gave me a queer feeling to be in the woods in midwinter with a lantern at five o'clock in the morning, a mile and a half from home. Nothing looked as it did in daylight, but I knew the marks I had made on trees, and there were big stumps and windfalls that I remembered. I had to be careful, however, noting every turn or half turn I made.

I was snaring snowshoe rabbits to sell. That morning I caught four and a partridge, and the partridge was a complete surprise; I didn't know one could get into a snare. I needed to be in the woods so early because I had some chores to do at home, and then I had to walk two miles to school at Orangedale.

I left home that day earlier than usual because I had to sell my rabbits to Burnt Jim, who lived conveniently close by the railway station. Burnt Jim wasn't admired by very many people, for he sold whiskey illegally, and probably with a lot of water in it. His family didn't like the business any more than other people did, but Burnt Jim was a law unto himself and did as he pleased.

That morning he was not in the little building where I usually found him, and so I went to the front door of his home, pulled the rabbits out of the sack as I went. One of Burnt Jim's nice-looking daughters answered my rap; she almost screamed the words, "We don't by rabbits!" and then slammed the door. I was wondering what to do with my catch when "Fog-horn" who always stayed at Burnt Jim's home came around the corner of the house and said in a voice that justified his name, "My boy, you'll catch hell if the women see those." But just then I saw Burnt Jim beckoning to me by the little house where he mixed things. Sometimes when you are in a spot, someone comes to your rescue by beckoning with his finger. Burnt Jim gave me forty cents for the rabbits and begged me to bring him all I could catch. I never found out where he sold them; no one we ever knew ate rabbits unless they were very short of food.

Burnt Jim was built like a turnip. He was fat and wheezed, and he wore a long white chin whisker. But I liked him, for he was always nice to me, and he bought the things I had to sell. He not only bought rabbits, but all the empty bottles and flasks that I could bring in—three cents for a big bottle if it had a good cork and two cents if it had no cork. Flasks with corks brought two cents, and without corks, one. I found the bottles along the railroad and in any place where men drank.

Up the Barren Road the spruce were tall and had no limbs for twenty feet or more, which made them very difficult to climb, but Duncan Dan and I tackled two that stood close together. We could see that they were full of hardened drops of gum that would be easy to pick once we got to them. Picking gum was fun, and while school was on at Orangedale, the gum had some economic value. We wrapped our legs around the trunks, pumped ourselves up, and began filling our mouths with the gum. It tasted pitchy at first, but after some chewing and spitting it was delicious.

As we climbed higher and higher, Duncan started talking again about our becoming ministers, and said his mother had had a dream about us. Something good had happened to him in the dream, but she dreamed that I was crucified like Jesus. "That must mean you're going to be the great and famous man," he said. I thought I would rather not be famous if I had to be crucified for it. Dreams, I thought, went opposite to what would really happen, and so I thought I'd likely not be crucified for anything. But the important point in Duncan's mind was that the dream seemed to indicate that we were right in planning to be ministers.

In my pocket were several empty gun-cap boxes. We filled three boxes this time, and we'd get three cents apiece for them. We sold this carefully processed and packaged gum to the bigger boys who usually had pennies, and one day the teacher caught me making a sale during school hours. She asked me if I had chewed the gum. "Yes," I said, "that gets the pitch out." She made a face as she gave the box back to me, and told me to keep it in my pocket. I didn't think she was very polite.

The air was cool one early dawn, but still there was the unmistakable smell of spring. The ice in the cove was partly broken up and the streams were clear, and the muskrats had started to go home after their swimming rambles. And that is what I was after—muskrats or "musquash" as many called them. Merchant Dan was paying twenty-five cents a pelt for them, and I needed the money very much. It's rather awful not to have any money at all, not even enough to buy a pencil, and so I wasn't inclined to miss a chance to earn an honest penny. Everyone was wearing a fur-lined coat in winter or wanted to, and so there was quite a demand for spring muskrat pelts.

I had a few traps along the shores of the river, set in the entrances to the muskrat's dens in the banks. I did not go to see my traps right away; it was too early for that. Besides, there was something about the morning that made me feel good, and feeling good is worth taking some time out to do. I walked along the railroad tracks to Monroe's Bridge about a half mile away and watched the muskrats swimming about, making long V's in the quiet water. Two muskrats swam side by side under the bridge where I stood, and they seemed to be talking to each other, or maybe scolding each other. I thought they were beautiful, but I did not dare let that feeling get hold of me because it would make me unwilling to kill them, and I started thinking of how much money I would make if I had a lot more traps. I suspected I was squeamish, and that was an awful thought. I remembered once when I tried to get away when the men were butchering hogs, and someone had said, "The kid's scared." Then I thought of the muskrats I had trapped, and of the times I found just a chewed-off leg in a trap.

One senses at such times that his mind is trying hard to tell him something important. That is how it was with me, but I shut off whatever was trying to communicate with me. I was the best muskrat-skinner around, better than any of the men; I could remove a pelt without disturbing even an eyelash. Father said once that I would make a good surgeon. I almost studied medicine later, and nothing but my lack of funds saved a lot of people who might have fallen into my hands.

I was watching from the bridge when two larger animals appeared in the water. They swam very fast, and all the muskrats disappeared as though they had melted away. The large animals were otters. I tried to get near them, but they anticipated every move I made, and made off in some other direction.

Then I spent some time listening to a bird we called the skylark; really it was a snipe that always flew at dawn and dusk, making lovely sounds with its wings as it dived from great heights and then flew up again. It went "ho ho ho ho ho ho ho," the sound getting very loud as the bird descended and then fading out as it ascended once more. That was the first bird I ever loved, and my feeling for it was like a religious veneration. I have heard birds that were supposed to be the same kind in other parts of the world, but none of them could hold a candle to this one.

It was time now to go home and check my traps, and before long I was skinning musquash, nauseated by their ugly carcasses. In some parts of the world people eat muskrat as a great delicacy. We didn't know about that, but I doubt we would have tried them even if we had known. There was something in the Bible that Father used to quote, about animals being edible if they had cloven hooves or chewed their cud, but I am sure that was not the reason why we didn't eat muskrat—it was related to one's feeling about eating dogs and cats.

Muskrats built reed houses on the creek flats above the old mill dam, and I had the bright idea of catching spring rats all winter and saving the pelts until spring. I cut holes in the tops of the rat houses and put the traps inside. The muskrats I caught that way gave me a feeling for which I had no name at the time, but it wasn't a happy feeling.

I finally graduated to the use of firearms, and John's old muzzle-loader shot gun was available. It had a broken stock which was held together with rabbit-snare wire. One evening when I came home I found Alan running up and down the river bank with an old gun, almost exhausted. He drew my attention to a muskrat swimming upstream that had been playing tricks with him. When he ran upstream to a point from which he could shoot, the clever animal turned around before he got there and started downstream again, but when he ran downstream to a gap in the bushes the rat went upstream again, and that had been going on for some time. Then I played a clever trick. I urged him to give me the gun, saying that I would stay right there behind the big old pine stump while he ran upstream again to make the rat return and that I would be ready for it. Alan knew he was being deceived but was too tired to protest just then, and so he went limping off once more. The rat turned as expected, and when it came opposite me I took careful aim and pulled the trigger. The gun went off like a cannon, at the same instant my neck and shoulders hit the ground with a thud and I lost consciousness. I was coming to when Alan came back, and I asked him who in hell had loaded the gun. He said Colin had said he couldn't remember whether or not he had put powder in when he was about to spill in the shot and so had put another charge of

124

powder in to make sure. "And I had to do the shooting!" I moaned. "That was a dirty trick you played on me," Alan replied. "Maybe the Devil put that extra kick in the gun as a judgment on you. I don't think your aim was so good anyhow." As he walked away I realized that I had missed the rat and I felt pleased and annoyed at the same time.

The muskrat pelts served a very real need at a critical time in my life. Like everything else, they went to merchant Dan, except that Mother insisted that I be personally paid in cash for them; my muskrats would have nothing to do with the family debt. Merchant Dan was a very gracious man and as honest as men are made, which was most fortunate for Mother.

The grown boys helped in the family. John often paid for flour and oatmeal and even clothing at times. Once he brought me a pair of shoes he was given as part payment by an employer who went broke. They were three sizes too big, but nevertheless I prized them greatly.

Once Neil who was working in the quarries at Marble Mountain, came home for a weekend and presented each of us with a fine suit of clothes. Mine was a double-breasted one and filled me with pride. These were the first "store suits" we ever owned.

Occasional purchases, however, didn't do much to relieve Mother's anxiety. She kept worrying about the farm being lost to merchant Dan and sometimes did so out loud for Father's benefit, at which times he either got angry or played deaf. Then one afternoon when he retorted sharply, she laid into him in real earnest. She couldn't take it any longer, she said; if he didn't go and settle with merchant Dan she would go herself, and that wouldn't be to his credit in the neighborhood. He roared her into silence, but all the same he put on his good coat, stamping the floor with little nervous steps as he did so, and then went out and started for Orangedale. A funeral silence fell upon us as he left. Mother couldn't believe he had gone, but at the same time she feared it was too late in any case—the business with merchant Dan had been going on for twenty years without any accounting.

During the next two or three hours Mother worked at her tasks with unusual deliberation. She spoke quietly to us with an air of resignation; she was prepared for the worst. We youngsters couldn't do anything but pace up and down and grin wryly at each other. Mother's fear had finally spread to us, and we began watching for Father's return before an hour was up. Katie seemed to be the only one who felt hopeful. "Maybe we're rich," she said, and when she received scornful looks from the rest of us she added, "Well, who knows? Why think the worst has happened?"

After what seemed an endless stretch of time, Flora shouted from upstairs that there was a peddlar coming; she could see him passing Uncle Hector's old shop. Everyone went to the window, and then several said at once, "It's Pa!" He was coming down the hill with an enormous bundle on his back. It was heavy but he was obviously in a hurry, for now and then he would take a few running steps. Then Colin said, "He's bought a lot of things, and that means . . . " Mother began to smile and weep both at once, and all the rest of us broke into roars of shouting and laughter.

When Father got to the house he had difficulty getting the bundle through the door, and then he spilled everything out onto the floor—shoes, clothing, suits of underwear, and many packages with unknown contents. "There you are," he said, "and we have twenty dollars to the good!" Mother said, "Oh, the honest man!" and then she did something that amazed us. She caught an end of Father's mustache in each hand and gave him a real kiss in the middle of the mouth. We were not a kissing family, and even Father was so startled that he looked like a boy being kissed for the first time.

That was when the great fear left us.

TITLES BY PETHERIC PRESS

The McKay Motor Car — W. H. McCurdy
The Bottle Collector — Azor Vienneau
Nova Scotia Furniture — G. E. G. MacLaren
Antique Potteries of Nova Scotia — G. E. G. MacLaren
The Story of The Nova Scotia Tartan — Marjorie Major
A Pocketful of Nova Scotia History — No. 1 — Joseph Howe
Silversmiths and Related Craftsmen
    of the Atlantic Provinces — Donald C. Mackay
Vanishing Halifax — L. B. Jenson
Nova Scotia Sketchbook — L. B. Jenson
Wood and Stone — L. B. Jenson
Country Roads — L. B. Jenson
The River that Missed the Boat — Barbara Grantmyre
Daveys Pilots and the Sea Wolves — Catherine L. Brown
Gaskill's Cove — R. B. Powell
God and the Devil at Seal Cove — A. H. MacLean

Also Publisher of

THE NOVA SCOTIA HISTORICAL QUARTERLY

PRINTED & BOUND
BY MCCURDY PRINTING CO. LTD
HALIFAX, NOVA SCOTIA, CANADA

127